SCHOLASTIC

QUICK TIPS! → Making the
First Six Weeks
a Success!

Grades K–5

KELLY BERGMAN

New York • Toronto • London • Auckland • Sydney
Mexico City • New Delhi • Hong Kong • Buenos Aires

Teaching *Resources*

To my parents—my original mentors: Thank you for helping me follow my dreams of teaching.

To my educational mentors: Thank you for all of your support as I have learned so much from each of you.

To my husband: Thank you for supporting me with my lofty goals.

To my daughters and nephews and nieces: Thank you for making me want to be the best teacher I can be.

To my sisters: Thank you for always being there for me.

 To customize and save the files on the CD, you will need to download Adobe Reader™, version 7.0 or higher. This download is available free of charge for Mac and PC systems at www.adobe.com/downloads.

Editor: Sarah Longhi

Content editor: Sarah Glasscock

Cover design by Maria Lilja

Interior design by Melinda Belter

ISBN-13: 978-0-545-16728-4

ISBN-10: 0-545-16728-0

Copyright © 2010 by Kelly Bergman

Contents

* Copies of these reproducibles appear in the book.
  Copies of all the reproducibles can be found on the CD.

* Copies of these reproducibles appear in the book.
  Copies of all the reproducibles can be found on the CD.

Introduction

I assumed my first mentoring role about one month after I started my first full-time teaching position. My own mentor had a baby in late September, and I became the mentor to her long-term substitute. A few years later, I was fortunate enough to be able to mentor a student teacher working in my classroom. Later, as an administrator, I oversaw student teachers in our building and mentored new teachers. As I've continued to work in education, each of my roles has included a mentoring component. I've finally realized that my niche in life is to mentor others and help them make sense of complex tasks.

Three years ago, I developed a one-day workshop to help teachers prepare for the first six weeks of school. I wanted to share my expertise and help make this process simpler for teachers. As I was creating the materials for the workshop, I decided that I wanted to be able to share the materials with a broader audience, thus the publication of this resource. It is a must for teachers who want to start the school year in an organized way and maintain that organization throughout the year.

If you're like most teachers, you tend to spend a lot of time doing administrative tasks, such as keeping track of information and materials. You've probably wished you could have spent that time planning or teaching instead. This book provides teacher-tested ideas and tools that will help simplify your life and help you feel confident throughout the year so that you can focus on instruction.

How to Use This Book · · · · · · · ·

Each chapter begins with two scenarios: Scenario A describes a day in the life of a teacher who is overwhelmed. Scenario B describes the same day as it's experienced by a teacher who is organized. (Someone who has read this book!) The next section, Tips for Success, introduces the main topics in the chapter. It's followed by the Tools for Success section, which discusses the reproducibles that go with the chapter. Take Action, the final section in the chapter, suggests practical next steps.

Each reproducible has an icon in the upper left-hand corner so you can easily identify whether it is designed for your use, for students, or for parents:

 Teacher reproducible

 Student reproducible

 Parent reproducible

If you are an experienced teacher, I suggest that you browse through the table of contents to select the sections that are most relevant to you. In addition, you may want to skim each chapter to view the thumbnail sketches of the reproducible templates. I'm guessing you'll find some that will make your life easier. I discuss each one in the Tools for Success section of every chapter. All reproducibles are included on the CD, ready to print. For your convenience, most teacher and parent reproducible files can be filled in onscreen and saved to your hard drive.

If you are a new teacher, I suggest that you read this book from cover to cover and complete each of the suggested tasks. New teachers that I've worked with have loved being able to walk through each step of this process and feel confident about starting the school year.

Throughout the book you will also find a variety of tips. These are suggestions that I have found to be very helpful and want to pass along to you. As with the entire book, my goal is to provide suggestions, tools, and tips to make your life easier.

To customize and save the files on the CD, you will need to download Adobe Reader™, version 7.0 or higher. This download is available free of charge for Mac and PC systems at

www.adobe.com/products/downloads

Chapter 1

Get to Know Your School and What's Expected of You

Scenario A You're a brand new teacher or new to a school. When you walk into your classroom, you're immediately overwhelmed because you don't know where to begin. Thoughts crowd your mind: *What will I put on my walls? How will I arrange my desks? What are the routines for lunch and recess? Where do I pick my students up when they arrive?* All of a sudden, you're so anxious that you don't know where to begin.

Scenario B You're a brand new teacher or new to a school. You walk in with a checklist in hand, and you hit the ground running. One of the first tasks on your checklist is to talk with the secretaries to learn more about the school's policies and procedures so you'll understand the lunch/recess schedule and the specials schedule. Then you move to the next task on your list. By the time you've checked off all the items on your checklist, you feel like you know a lot about the school's policies and procedures, and you're ready to focus on your classroom.

Tips for Success • • • • • • • • •

Learn About School Policies and Procedures Learning as much as you can about the school you're working in is critical—whether you're a new teacher or an experienced one starting in a new school. The more you know about how the school operates and what is expected of you as a member of its staff, the better you'll perform.

Make Decisions About Your Classroom Using This Information
Once you've learned as much as you can about your school, you can move to the decisions you need to make in your classroom. For example, you have to know the schoolwide schedule for lunch and recess before you can make your daily schedule. You have to know the school policy on snacks and water bottles before you can make decisions about them for your own classroom. Then you can move forward and make decisions for your classroom that will support school policies.

TOOLS FOR SUCCESS

The To-Do Lists in this chapter are designed to help you learn the intricate details of how your school works and the basic daily tasks you're expected to do. Each of the following templates appears on the CD (see CD, Chapter 1 folder). Type information into each template, print it, and save it to use again.

TO-DO LIST Before School Starts This first list includes tasks that should be done before school starts because they will guide the decisions you make for setting up your classroom. Examples of tasks on this list include the following:

- *Learn about the school's emergency procedures.* You may discover that you must keep a current class list near the door of the classroom. Many teachers staple a folder that contains the class list right next to the door where they can grab it easily in case of a drill or an actual emergency evacuation.

- *Learn lunch procedures—find out how the lunch count is taken.* Knowing the time and accounting details of this procedure will enable you to factor it into your morning routine.

(pages 12–14; CD folder *Chapter1*)

TO-DO LIST First Two Weeks of School The second list includes tasks that need to be done during the first two weeks of school—once you've established your classroom and your students have arrived. Now you need to start planning for the next stages of the school year. Examples of tasks on this list include the following:

- *Return to the first checklist and add any tasks that still need to be accomplished.* Make sure to wrap up any remaining items from the Before School Starts list.

- *Make phone calls to each set of parents to tell them something positive that you've noticed about their child.* Making these phone calls lays a critical foundation for positive relationships with parents.

(page 15; CD folder *Chapter1*)

TO-DO LIST **First Month of School** The third list includes tasks that need to be done during the first month of school. The main task is to prepare for Parent Conferences. By now, your class has settled into its routines, and it's time to start thinking about conferences with parents and planning for the next few months. This To-Do list and other tools within this book help make sure that you are ready for productive conferences with parents. Since a conference is held during a short period of time, you want to make sure that you're prepared for each one.

(page 16; CD folder *Chapter1*)

 TO-DO LIST **First Six Weeks of School** The final list in this chapter outlines tasks that can be done once the year has started, and you've held your first round of parent conferences. The primary task on this list is to find out about field trip policies in your school. Chances are that you'll have a field trip coming up, so you'll want to make sure you know how to plan for it.

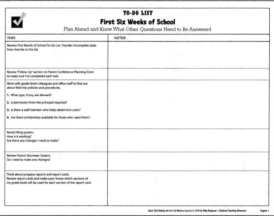

(page 17; CD folder *Chapter1*)

Kelly's Tip

When working through the To-Do lists, keep in mind that most staff and resource people will allow you to drop in and talk to them, but offering to make an appointment shows that you respect their time. This important gesture ensures that you start your relationships on a good note.

Take Action ··············

■ Review the first To-Do List on page 12. You'll see that each list has three columns. The first column lists the task, the second column provides space for you to take notes as you talk to your resource people, and the third column gives the location of related resources in this book. You have everything in one place and can refer back to the information as needed.

■ Fill in the pieces of information that you already know.

■ Schedule appointments with your resource people to fill in the pieces of information that you don't know.

■ Use this information as you develop your classroom procedures and routines.

■ Periodically review each list. Make notes next to the outstanding questions to confirm that you know whom to talk to about each question and schedule appointments with those people.

■ Develop a good organizational habit by keeping the To-Do Lists on a clipboard. (See Chapter 2 for more about using a clipboard to keep important information organized.)

TO-DO LIST
Before School Starts
Learn as Much as You Can About Your School

TASK	NOTES	REFERENCE IN BOOK
Mark Back to School Night/Curriculum Night on calendar. Find out: **1.** Is it done as a team or individually? **2.** What is expected of me?	1. Done individually 2. Must discuss reading, writing, math, social studies, science, homework routines	Back to School Night/Curriculum Night Agenda: Chapter 7, page 48
Learn attendance procedures. Find out: **1.** By what time is it needed? _9am_ **2.** Is it manual or electronic? **3.** If manual, how/where is it turned in? **4.** What is tardy policy? **5.** How are late arrivals/early dismissals handled? **6.** Do I keep track of my own attendance? _no_ **7.** What is policy for trips? **8.** What is policy for make-up work?	1. Office needs by 9am 2. Done electronically 4. Tardy students must bring orange slip from office to show they checked in. 5. To pick up student before school is dismissed, parent must go to office to sign child out; office will call classroom to request student. 6. Office keeps track of attendance.	Absentee Make-Up Work Form, Chapter 3 page 27

Sample To-Do List

TO-DO LIST
Before School Starts
Learn as Much as You Can About Your School

TASK	NOTES	REFERENCE IN BOOK
Complete Classroom Inventory.		Classroom Inventory: Chapter 2, page 21
Put school and district dates in calendar/plan book/personal device.		
Introduce myself to office staff, custodial staff, and resource people (ESL, GT, etc.).		
Ask about Staff and/or Parent Handbooks and read them thoroughly.		
Review Teacher Supply List.		Teacher Supply List: Chapter 2, page 23
Mark Back to School Night/Curriculum Night on calendar. Find out: **1.** Is it done as a team or individually? **2.** What is expected of me?		Back to School Night/Curriculum Night Agenda: Chapter 7, page 48
Learn attendance procedures. Find out: **1.** By what time is it needed? _____ **2.** Is it manual or electronic? **3.** If manual, how/where is it turned in? **4.** What is tardy policy? **5.** How are late arrivals/early dismissals handled? **6.** Do I keep track of my own attendance? _____ **7.** What is policy for trips? **8.** What is policy for make-up work?		Absentee Make-Up Work Form, Chapter 3 page 27
Learn lunch count procedures.		

TASK	NOTES	REFERENCE IN BOOK
Learn clinic procedures. Find out: **1.** Which students need medication? **2.** Where are clinic passes?		Clinic Pass: Chapter 2, page 22
Learn emergency procedures.		
Learn library procedures. Find out: **1.** How do teachers check out books? **2.** How do teachers work with Librarian/Library Media Specialist? **3.** Can individual students go to library any time during the day? **4.** Do students need to be accompanied by an adult? **5.** Do classes visit library on a weekly basis, or are they scheduled as needed? **6.** Do students check out their own books, or do adults do this? **7.** Do students need an ID or a number to check out books? **8.** How long can students keep books? **9.** What happens if books are lost?		Library Pass: Chapter 2, page 22
Review report card to learn format/topics covered. Find out: **1.** How often are report cards sent home? **2.** Does school use formal progress reports? If so, how often are they done? **3.** What sort of grading scale is used? **4.** Are absences included in report cards? If so, do I keep track of absences, or does office?		

TASK	NOTES	REFERENCE IN BOOK
Establish homework policies and routines. Find out: 1. When will homework be sent home (nightly, once a week, etc.)? 2. When will homework be due? 3. Will I have a set routine every week or will it vary depending on work done in class?		Sample Homework Contracts: Chapter 4, page 34
Determine how/when work will be sent home. Find out: 1. Does school have a set day of the week when letters are sent home? 2. Will I use "Friday Folders"? If so, how/where will I file work and papers during the week?		
Learn proper paper heading. (How should students write their names on their papers?)		
Get copy of daily schedule for my class. (Know when specials, lunch/recess, etc. are scheduled.)		
Find out if students may have snacks and/or water bottles in class. 1. If permitted, when will I let students have them? 2. How will I teach students about proper use of water bottles? 3. How will I teach students about healthy snacks?		
Review students' supply lists. (Decide how each item will be used.)		First Week Planning Tools: Chapter 6, pages 46–47
Identify students on my roster with health issues/special needs.		Learning Plan Goal Sheet: Chapter 5, page 43
Make passes: bathroom, clinic, library.		Sample Passes: Chapter 2, page 22 Bathroom Sign-Out/Sign-In, Chapter 4, page 33

TO-DO LIST

First Two Weeks of School

Continue to Learn as Much as You Can About Your School and Settle Into Your Classroom Routines

TASK	NOTES	REFERENCE IN BOOK
Review Before School Starts To-Do List. Transfer incomplete tasks from that list to this list.		
1. Do I have all important school dates on my calendar?		
2. Have I read all Staff and/or Parent Handbooks?		
3. Do I have a clear understanding of emergency procedures?		
4. Have I reviewed school report card?		
Set up voice mail. Include the following:		
1. Name		
2. Grade level		
3. Time that messages are checked each day		
4. Amount of time it will take to return calls ("I will return your call within 24 hours.")		
Set up e-mail files. Include files for the following:		
1. Principal		
2. Parents		
3. Colleagues		
Make positive phone calls to parents at home.		Parent Communication Log, Chapter 9, page 60
1. What are one or two things that I've noticed the child doing well these first few days of school?		Back to School Night/Curriculum Night Agenda, Chapter 7, page 48
2. Is Back to School Night/Curriculum Night coming up? Remind parents about important upcoming events.		
3. Tell parents the best way to contact me (phone number and time).		
Are there any staff members that I haven't yet connected with? Be sure I have met all my resource people.		

TO-DO LIST

First Month of School

Start Thinking About Conferences

TASK	NOTES	REFERENCE IN BOOK
Review First Two Weeks To-Do List. Transfer incomplete tasks from that list to this list. • Have I made a positive phone call to each child's parent or caretaker?		Parent Communication Log, Chapter 9, page 60
If I plan to use parent volunteers in my classroom, decide how to use volunteers and schedule them to come into classroom.		Parent Volunteer Form, Chapter 7, page 53 Parent Volunteer Tips, Chapter 7, page 53
Take a few minutes to make sure I'm using most effective instructional strategies. Are there new ideas I can integrate?		Study Tips, Chapter 10, pages 67–69 Instructional Strategies, Appendix, page 70
Prepare for substitute teachers.		Prepare for a Substitute Teacher, Chapter 8, page 54
Ask about requirements for conferences. Find out: **1.** Are they teacher-led or student-led? **2.** Are they required or optional?		Chapter 10
Find out how conferences are scheduled. **1.** Do I schedule them? _____ **2.** Are they scheduled by office? _____		Parent Conference Scheduling Form, Chapter 10, page 64
Determine whether students attend conferences with parents.		
Communicate with parents to schedule conferences and inform them about expectations (teacher-led or student-led, required or optional, whether children attend).		Parent Conference Letter, Chapter 10, page 64
Begin collecting student work samples to share at conferences.		Start Your Filing System, Chapter 2, page 19
What will I have available for parents to look at while they wait for their conference? **1.** Do I have books that my class has made and parents can read while they wait? **2.** Does my school subscribe to any parenting magazines? **3.** Are there school, district, and/or PTA newsletters that I could have available? **4.** Are there any recent articles about success stories in my school?		
Complete a Parent Conference Planning Sheet for each student.		Parent Conference Planning Sheet, Chapter 10, page 65

TO-DO LIST

First Six Weeks of School

Plan Ahead and Know What Other Questions Need to Be Answered

TASK	NOTES	REFERENCE IN BOOK
Review First Month of School To-Do List. Transfer incomplete tasks from that list to this list.		
Review "Follow Up" section on Parent Conference Planning Sheet to make sure I've completed each task.		Chapter 10, page 65
Work with grade-level colleagues and office staff to find out about field trip policies and procedures. **1.** What type, if any, are allowed? **2.** Is permission from the principal required? **3.** Is there a staff member who helps determine costs? **4.** Are there scholarships available for those who need them?		
Revisit filing system. How is it working? Are there any changes I need to make?		Start Your Filing System, Chapter 2, page 19
Review Parent Volunteer System. Do I need to make any changes?		Parent Volunteer Form and Tips, Chapter 7, page 53
Think about progress reports and report cards. Review report cards and make sure I know which sections of my grade book will be used for each section of the report card.		

Get Organized and Stay Organized

Scenario A You're exhausted after your third day of school. You went in early to stand in line at the copy machine to make some copies. (You didn't have time to get them ready for the Copy Aide.) A student didn't feel well. While you were searching for a piece of paper to write a note to the Clinic Aide, the class got disruptive, and it took 10 minutes to get them refocused. You need to make a couple of phone calls to parents to ask about some medical issues, but you realize that you don't have their phone numbers at home. You crawl into bed early.

Scenario B You're relaxing with a sense of satisfaction after the third day of school. Because you've been very efficient in getting your materials ready for the Copy Aide, you haven't had to do any copying yourself. A student didn't feel well, and you wrote the Clinic Pass so efficiently that the class kept working and didn't realize you were doing something else. You have a couple of quick phone calls to make to parents. Their names and phones numbers are at your fingertips, so it will be easy to make the calls. You have enough energy to complete a couple of tasks before bed.

Getting organized before school starts will be worth a million dollars on the day students arrive. If you take time to get your calendar ready, establish a filing system, make copies of the forms you'll need, and get to know your resource people, you will have developed an organizational system that will allow you to easily handle the daily operations of a classroom.

Kelly's Tip
If you allow students to get off task for as little as 30 seconds, it will take about 10 minutes to reestablish a learning environment. Have your passes readily available so you don't have to take time to search for them. This will allow you to handle interruptions without letting students get off task.

Tips for Success · · · · · · · · · ·

Get Your Calendar Ready How will you keep your calendar? Will you do so electronically or on a hard copy? Will you have a personal calendar and a school calendar—or will you keep one calendar? As soon as you get into your school, get copies of your school and district calendars. Transfer all the important dates onto your calendar so you know well in advance when the important events are.

Kelly's
Tip Keep one calendar with both personal and school dates on it. By doing this, you will only have to check one calendar when you are scheduling appointments. Using a single calendar also minimizes the chances of scheduling errors.

Start Your Filing System Begin with a small but efficient color-coded filing system. This filing system has three sections: (1) Individual Months, (2) Instruction/Management/Record Keeping, and (3) Individual Students.

INDIVIDUAL MONTHS
Choose one color (blue, for example) and create a folder for each month of the school year. As you come across ideas for Valentine's Day, you can quickly file them in the February folder. If you know you have a field trip coming up in November, you can file any information about it in the November folder.

INSTRUCTION/MANAGEMENT/RECORD KEEPING
Next, choose a different color (yellow, for example) and create the following folders for instruction, management, and record-keeping:

Back to School Night/Curriculum Night As you gather materials for this big event, you can quickly file them in this folder. When you make copies of materials for parents, make a few extra copies to keep in this folder. When new students arrive in your classroom, you can easily locate a copy of the material to send home with him or her (along with a welcome letter—see Chapter 3) so those parents/caretakers have the same information as the parents/caretakers of your other students do.

Kelly's
Tip Prepare packets of information for Back To School Night/Curriculum Night. These packets might include copies of the following; daily schedule, homework policies (see Chapter 4), and reading strategies (see Chapter 10). Write students' names on the first page of the packets so you know which parents attended your event. Send packets home to families who weren't able to attend.

Parent Conferences As you collect materials for conferences, keep them in this file so you can access the information easily when you prepare for conferences.

Weekly Bulletins and/or School Newsletters Read every piece of information that is sent home to parents so you know everything they know. Keep copies of bulletins and school newsletters in this folder to easily refer back to them if you need to.

Classroom Newsletter (see Chapter 9) You never know when you might need an extra copy of a newsletter or want to refer back to one. It's also helpful to send these home to new families so they can see what's been going on before they arrived.

Blank Class Lists Type the names of your students in the first column of a blank Class List sheet and make several copies. You will be amazed at the number of times you need a blank class list; for example, you might devote columns to collecting field trip money, keeping track of participation in activities, and so on.

New Students Chapter 3 includes materials to make sure that you are ready when new students arrive in your classroom. Keep copies of appropriate materials in this folder.

INDIVIDUAL STUDENTS

Finally, choose a third color of file folder (green, for example) and create a file for each student. Keep notes from parents, clinic passes, student work samples, and so on in these folders. You can access a lot of information about a student by referring back to his or her folder. Retain these files for one full year after the students have moved on to the next grade, just in case you need to refer back to them.

Now you have a filing system that is easy to use. If you have something to file in the January folder, you can go to your blue folders and easily find the January folder. If you need to find something for parent conferences, you can look in the yellow folders and find the one labeled "Parent Conferences."

TOOLS FOR SUCCESS

As teachers, we want to focus on instruction. We sometimes forget that there are many, many "little details" each day in our classroom that take our focus away from instruction. The tools in this chapter are designed to make your life in the classroom more efficient. Each of the following templates is on the CD (see CD, Chapter 2 folder).

Kelly's Tip
Keep important information on a clipboard that you can have with you at all times. This is a good place to keep a copy of the Class Information Form, student health plans, and Learning Plan Goal Sheets (discussed in Chapter 5). I also suggest that you keep your To-Do Lists on this clipboard until they are completed.

Class Information Form When you meet your students and their families for the first time, have them provide you with some basic contact information. You might use the Student Information Card in Chapter 5 to collect this information. Then you can use the completed forms to compile the information onto this one-page form.

Kelly's
Tip Use the Student Information Card in Chapter 5 to compile the Class Information List. The card asks parents/caretakers to identify the first and second contacts for their children. This allows you to communicate with parents/caretakers in the manner they have requested, allowing for more efficient communication.

Keep one copy of the Class Information Form at school (on your clipboard) and one at home. You will always have contact information at your fingertips and won't have to spend time searching for it.

Class List Fill in your students' names in the first column and make several copies to keep in your files. You'll find yourself using this class list in a variety of ways, such as recording students' behavior by using checkmarks for misbehavior; keeping track of when students turn assignments in and when you meet with them for a one-on-one writing conference; logging in field trip permission slips; and handing out copies to make sure that each student gives a Valentine's card to every other student in the class.

Finally, consider posting a class list with your emergency information near the exit door so you can grab it on your way out.

Classroom Inventory It's important to know what materials are in your classroom when you arrive. This form will allow you to keep an accurate list of school materials and your personal materials.

Clinic Pass This pass has been carefully designed to provide important information, including the time the student leaves the classroom and the time he or she leaves the clinic. This way, students know they are expected to go straight to the clinic and then straight back to class. If you complete this pass each time you send a student to the clinic and you file returned passes in students' individual files, you will have useful data about your students.

For instance, you may wonder about a student who's visiting the clinic often. You can go back and review his or her clinic passes and notice that this student has been having a lot of stomachaches. You might need to talk to the student's parents to find out why these stomachaches might be happening—perhaps there have been changes in the child's life. You might learn that the student gets ill at the same time each day—perhaps that student is struggling with writing and goes to the clinic to avoid writing. You might also use a student's clinic passes to start a dialogue with the clinic aide/nurse or administrators to make sure that others are watching out for that child, too.

Copy Request Form Teachers spend an incredible amount of time and hundreds of sticky notes writing notes to request copies. Fill in your name, make copies of the Copy Request Form, and cut it into fourths. When you need copies, complete the form, clip it to the original, and you're ready to go. *Note:* SS means single-sided and DS means double-sided.

Library Pass The Library Pass was also specially designed to include some important information. Notice that you fill in the reason for the library visit. This helps the student remember the reason for visiting the library, and it helps the adult in the library understand the purpose of the visit. The pass includes times when the student leaves the classroom and the library to prevent anyone from spending too much time in the halls.

Kelly's Tip
Color code your passes and forms. For instance, your Clinic Passes may be blue, Library Passes may be green, etc. This will make it even easier for you to grab a pass while you continue to teach.

Kelly's Tip
A timer allows you to keep your classroom moving efficiently. If you tell students that they have 10 minutes to work on an activity and you set your timer for 10 minutes, you can focus on working with students instead of watching the clock.

☑ Teacher Supply List New teachers frequently ask for a list of supplies necessary to start the school year. This list is divided into "Must Have" and "Nice to Have." Check to see which of these materials the school supplies before spending your own money on them.

Kelly's Tip

Inexpensive rubber dishpans come in very handy in the classroom. Label one dishpan for each day of the week. As you prepare materials, place them in the appropriate dishpan so you have all your materials ready for each day. This task is especially helpful when you have a substitute teacher. If your school has wire baskets, you can use them for the same purpose. Another, cheaper, and "greener" option is cardboard trays that hold beverage six-packs.

☑ Teacher Supply List

MUST HAVE
- ☐ Chalk/Whiteboard markers
- ☐ Eraser
- ☑ Stapler
- ☐ Clear tape
- ☐ Masking tape
- ☑ File folders (preferably a variety of colors)
- ☐ Sticky notes
- ☐ Paper clips
- ☐ Plan book
- ☐ Timer
- ☐ Dishpans, baskets, or soda trays to organize materials

_____
_____
_____

NICE TO HAVE
- ☐ Device for playing music (Consider playing classical music as students arrive and while they write.)
- ☑ Other
  Bookshelf

Sample Teacher Supply List

Take Action · · · · · · · · · · · ·

- ■ Before you unpack any of your things, complete the Classroom Inventory template so you know what materials were in your classroom when you arrived. File this in your August folder.

- ■ Put all school and district dates on your calendar.

- ■ Begin gathering the materials on the Teacher Supply List.

- ■ Set up your filing system.

- ■ Fill in your name on the passes before you copy them. You'll save a few seconds of time by not having to write your name each time you fill in a pass.

- ■ Choose colors for your passes and then make your copies.

- ■ Find a place to keep your passes so you can easily access them—perhaps a little organizer on your desk or a desk drawer.

- ■ Get to know your resource people. Who are the support people in your building? What kinds of support do they provide?

- ■ After you've collected contact information for each student, compile your Class Information Form.

Chapter 3

Establish Your Classroom Environment for Optimal Learning

Scenario A The principal brought the new student to your classroom, and you were embarrassed by what she saw. While you were trying to move about the classroom during the lesson, you couldn't get to parts of the room because of the tight arrangement of desks. In fact, several students bumped their chairs into each other trying to get up. Students got off task while you were meeting the new student, and it took almost three minutes to get their attention focused back on you. You had no place for the new student to sit and no idea what to do to welcome him. The principal was not pleased.

Scenario B The principal brought the new student to your classroom, and you were totally prepared. You were in the middle of a lesson, circulating easily around the room and making contact with each student. Thanks to your thoughtful arrangement of desks, there was plenty of space to work and move. Students quietly continued with the activity while you met with the principal and the new student. You had already selected a "buddy" for the new student and set an empty desk next to her desk. After introducing the two students, you had the new student set her belongings on her desk. You handed the New Student Orientation checklist to the "buddy" and sent the two students on their way to tour the school and get to know each other. You instantly got the attention of the rest of the class and continued with the activity while the principal watched with a smile.

Optimal instruction takes place in a classroom that is warm, focused, and well organized. Thinking about the room arrangement and planning for an easy-to-navigate space for students and teacher is an important part of classroom organization. Setting high expectations about behavior and work quality, and teaching students about these expectations, just as you would any other subject, helps to create a warm, focused classroom environment. Laying this foundation at the beginning of the school year creates a classroom where optimal learning takes place and where students want to be.

Kelly's Tip Begin the year by being stricter with students than you intend to be. While you're developing your classroom routines, be friendly but firm and absolutely consistent. As students get settled into the routines, you can loosen up slightly. It's always easier to loosen up than it is to tighten up.

Tips for Success • • • • • • • • • •

Arrange Your Classroom There are several questions that you must answer in order to arrange your classroom for optimum efficiency: Do you have desks or tables in your classroom? If you have desks, do you want them in rows or in groups? How many students do you want in each group? How can you arrange the desks so that all students can see the front of the classroom? Make sure that all students (including any in wheelchairs) can move easily through the classroom. Where will your desk be? Where will you meet with a large group? Where will you meet with small groups? What will you put on the walls? Draw a map to help you anticipate any problems in flow and movement and talk it over with a colleague.

Kelly's
Tip Place your desk so that you face the classroom door. You won't spend much time at your desk during the day, but you want to make sure that, for safety reasons, you can always see the door. If you happen to be working late after school, you want to make sure that you have full view of the door.

Select a Signal for Getting Students' Attention You want to be able to get students' attention immediately wherever you are in the classroom or school, so you need to think about what kind of signal to use. Some teachers clap their hands in a rhythm that students recognize and repeat; some say a couple of words and ask the students to respond as the suggestions below demonstrate; some raise their hands and wait for students to raise their hands. Choose one signal that you will use and practice it with students so that it works.

SUGGESTIONS FOR STUDENT RESPONSE

Teacher: One, two . . .   *Students:* eyes on you.
Teacher: Saylor Park . . . [school name]   *Students:* Panthers. [mascot]
Teacher: Do your . . .   *Students:* best.
Teacher: Time to . . .   *Students:* listen.

Set Classroom Rules Will you determine the classroom rules before students arrive or will they be involved in developing the rules? Focus on only a few key rules. Having a few rules sets a more positive tone for your classroom. Students can concentrate on learning instead of trying to remember a long set of rules, and you can focus on teaching instead of enforcement. Post the rules in your classroom for reinforcement.

Kelly's Tip Whether you develop the rules or students do, consider waiting to post them in the classroom for a couple days. Students are usually on their best behavior the first few days of school, and it sets a warmer tone when the rules are not the first thing they see. Also, you can incorporate examples of positive interactions you've already seen in your classroom.

Develop a Way to Handle Student Absences Think about how you will keep track of make-up work when students are absent. Consider placing a folder that says something like "We Missed You" on the desk of a student who is absent. Ask one student to be responsible for each absent student. Each time a paper is handed out, the assigned student can place the paper in the folder so that everything is in one place when the absent student returns to school. At the end of the day, take a few quick minutes to complete the Absentee Make-Up Work Form and place it in the folder.

Prepare to Welcome New Students and Support Those Who Move Away Part of a warm, caring learning environment is making sure that all students feel they are part of a learning community, regardless of when they join the group. Having a well-established plan for welcoming new students will allow them to quickly settle into the class. Consider giving new students a small "Introducing Me" bag to take home and fill with objects of their choice. They can bring the bag back to school and share their objects as a way of introducing themselves to the class.

Establishing a way to send off students who move during the school year is important to reduce their anxiety about moving and let them know they will be missed. It will also allow the rest of the class to recognize the change and achieve some closure.

Kelly's Tip Chapter 4 discusses the importance of having a morning routine that allows students to enter the classroom in a calm, organized way and begin a learning activity right away (see page 33). Once you have this routine in place, you can spend a few minutes while students are working to welcome back the student who was absent and briefly review the materials on his or her desk. You can also discuss with the student a time when the work can be made up.

TOOLS FOR SUCCESS

Optimal learning takes place in classrooms that have been carefully thought out and set up. In well-structured classrooms, all students feel welcome. The tools in this chapter are designed to help you establish an optimal learning environment in your classroom. Each of the following templates appears on the CD (see CD, Chapter 3 folder).

Absentee Make-Up Work Form If you haven't already created folders to hold work for students who are absent, take a few minutes to do that. At the end of each day, complete the Absentee Make-Up Work Form for each absentee (if more than one student is absent, you can fill out the form and then make copies of it). When completing the form, you can list topics covered, assignments that need to be made up, and any other notes that you want to be sure to tell the student.

Classroom Rules Ideas This sample shows ideas for grades K–2 and 3–5 classroom rules. As I mentioned earlier, aim for fewer rules rather than more rules. You can always add rules if necessary.

New Student Checklist Use this checklist to make sure that you have everything ready to welcome a new student into your classroom. Having everything ready for a new student will help him or her quickly feel comfortable in the new setting.

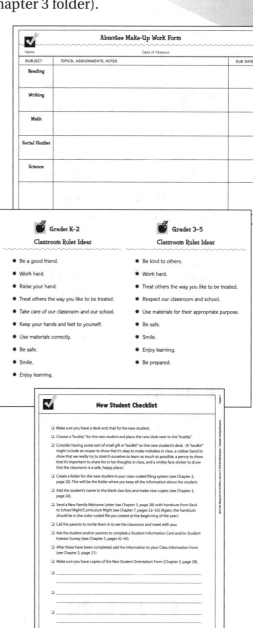

Kelly's Tip

Have students stand in a big circle and introduce themselves. Encourage students to tell one thing they like to do, so the new student can see what he or she has in common with the other students. Student volunteers can also explain the classroom rules and summarize what the class has been working on. Do a couple of these activities during the new student's first day and possibly repeat them for a couple of days.

New Student Orientation Form
After you have assigned a "buddy" to the new student, ask the "buddy" to take the new student on a tour of the school and to accomplish each of the tasks on the form. This is a friendly way to make sure that the new student has gotten a tour of the school and gets to meet the appropriate people. You can add or delete topics to customize this form to fit your school.

New Family Welcome Letter
Send this letter home with a copy of the packet from Back to School Night/Curriculum Night (in the folder you created in your filing system). It is a reassuring way to welcome families and make sure that they have your contact information. If the family does not speak English, ask the office staff about the availability of translation resources.

Student Moving Letter
Having a student leave the class during the middle of the school year is a change for all students. Be sure to find a way to send the student off in a way that provides closure for all.

Kelly's Tip
Creating a special gift or card for a student who moves away during the school year provides that student with a token of comfort during a time of transition. This could be as simple as having each student sign a card, or you could allow each student to make a card. If you have class pictures or other pictures of students, you may want to include those in some way.

Take Action · · · · · · · · · · · · ·

- Draw a map of your classroom. Explain to a colleague why you've arranged it the way that you have. This will help you talk through your decisions, anticipate possible problems, and generate new solutions.

- Decide what signal you will use to get students' attention.

- Make your decisions about classroom rules. Who will decide them? What will they be?

- Develop your plan for student absences.

Grades K–2

Classroom Rules Ideas

* Be a good friend.

* Work hard.

* Raise your hand.

* Treat others the way you like to be treated.

* Take care of our classroom and our school.

* Keep your hands and feet to yourself.

* Use materials correctly.

* Be safe.

* Smile.

* Enjoy learning.

Grades 3–5

Classroom Rules Ideas

* Be kind to others.

* Work hard.

* Treat others the way you like to be treated.

* Respect our classroom and school.

* Use materials for their appropriate purpose.

* Be safe.

* Smile.

* Enjoy learning.

* Be prepared.

Chapter 4

Develop Routines to Make Each Day a Productive One, From Arrival to Dismissal

Scenario A Students run into the classroom, tripping over each other. They toss their backpacks toward the coat rack and sprint to their seats. They talk and play while you visit with the parent who has stopped by. School has officially started, but the kids are still goofing around. Your day has gotten off to a hectic start, and the rest of the day continues to be chaotic. Student behavior is less than stellar, and several students choose to use the bathroom numerous times during the day. All of a sudden, it's time for students to go home, and you don't have the homework assignment ready. You're starting to wonder how you'll ever catch up.

Scenario B Classical music is playing in your classroom. You stand at the door to greet each student as he or she enters. Students come in quietly and hang their backpacks on the coat rack. They sharpen pencils, fill water bottles, and immediately get started on the morning activity you have written on the board. Students work quietly while you visit with the parent who has stopped by. Their behavior is certainly living up to the class expectations. As the day draws to a close, students know exactly what needs to be done before they can go home. You explained the homework packet to them this morning. Now you're ready to hand it out so students can put it in their backpacks. You stand at the door to say good-bye to each student. Your day went exactly as planned!

The way you start your day will determine the tone for the rest of the day. Develop a morning routine that allows students to enter the classroom and immediately begin learning. Maintain routines throughout the day so that students know what to expect and how to behave. End each day on a positive note and avoid the chaos that so frequently occurs at dismissal time.

Tips for Success · · · · · · · · · ·

Start the Learning the Minute Students Arrive Greeting students at the door as they arrive each day allows you to have a quick one-on-one interaction with each student before the class begins the morning routines. You also need to think about the morning chores that students will do (set out chairs, fill water bottles, sharpen pencils, make lunch choices, and so on).

Always have an activity ready for students to begin as soon as they've completed these arrival tasks. This will give you a few minutes to handle anything that comes up, and students will be immediately engaged in learning. Develop a consistent routine where students review the morning activity and complete it in a specific notebook, but be sure to include some variety in the activities themselves. On some mornings, a math activity may be written on the board; on other mornings, students may find a writing activity on a piece of paper on their desks. Sometimes, you may want to address kinesthetic intelligence (e.g., role play or pantomime); other times, you may want to address spatial intelligence (e.g., collage or flip book).

Kelly's Tip

The student supply list usually includes at least a couple of spiral notebooks. Consider labeling one of these "Morning Activities" so students have a consistent place to work on their morning activities. They should get out this notebook each morning when they finish their chores.

Keep the Learning Active Until the Minute Students Leave The end of the day seems to be one of the most chaotic times of the day. Think about how you can make this time of day calmer. Is it possible to have students get everything ready to go home and then read aloud to them for a few minutes before they leave? Be sure to factor into your schedule time for students to accomplish tasks (stack chairs, get papers out of a cubby or mailbox, gather backpacks and jackets, and so on). For instance, if school ends at 3:15, begin your dismissal routine at 2:55. Have students complete their tasks, put their backpacks on their desks, and meet in the large group area by 3:05. Read for 10 minutes until dismissal time and then have students get their backpacks while you stand at the door. Standing at the door to say good-bye gives you another opportunity to have a quick one-on-one interaction with each student. This may be as simple as a quick good-bye, or it might be a compliment, a reminder, or words of encouragement for a student who is struggling.

Establish Bathroom Procedures You will want to establish clear bathroom procedures for students. This is one more way to ensure that you spend the majority of your time on instruction rather than management. When will students be able to use the bathroom? How will they ask for permission to go (raise their hands, stand by the door, approach you to ask)? How will you remember who is out of the classroom? Will students have to sign out and in? One easy-to-manage approach to keeping track of students' bathroom use is a Sign-Out/Sign-In sheet that allows you to quickly see how many times the students are using the bathroom and when they're using it. If you think a student seems to be using the bathroom frequently, you can refer back to the Sign-Out/Sign-In Sheet to see that she has to go to the bathroom during math every day. This alerts you that the student may be having some issues in math that need to be addressed.

Kelly's Tip

Find an object for students to place on their desks when they go to the bathroom. In case of an emergency, you want to be able to quickly scan the classroom to see who is out of the room. Some teachers use a tennis ball container because it stands tall enough to be seen from anywhere in the classroom. Fill the container with a few rocks or something to give it a little weight and then cover it with brightly colored paper. Leave the container near the door so students can place it on their desks before they leave the room.

Keep Students on Task to Prevent Misbehavior Allowing time for students to get off task encourages misbehavior. Develop routines and transitions that allow little down time so that students are always focused on a task. For example, you might give students a mental math problem to solve while they put their supplies away and get new ones out, have students spell and define words while they line up, or tell them to touch their toes while they're standing in line. Keeping students focused on learning or using physical activities to give them a brain break, even during a very short period of time, helps you and them progress to the next part of the day's plans smoothly.

Develop Effective Homework Routines Homework should be an extension of the learning that took place in the classroom; it should not be new content. When developing homework routines, consider your needs as well as the needs of parents. What routine will you use so that you can get the best student response with homework? Will you send one homework packet home each week? Will you send it home on Monday and expect it back on Thursday? Will you send something home each night? If so, will you have a set schedule where you send math on Monday, spelling on Tuesday, and so on? Will you have a Homework Contract that students and parents sign? How will you grade homework? In your school, does homework have a separate place on the report card?

TOOLS FOR SUCCESS

Learning should begin the minute the students arrive, continue through the end of the day, and then be connected to the homework you send home. These tools are designed to assist with the development of daily routines so that you can focus on instruction. Each of the following templates appears on the CD (see CD, Chapter 4 folder).

Morning Activities You must be very organized in the morning and have the morning activity written on the board or displayed on the screen before students arrive. This tool, on pages 35–37, begins with a list of possible activities, then lists quotes that can be used to elicit responses from students. It then moves to multiple intelligence activities that you can use with different products for different areas of intelligence. These tools will allow you to quickly develop your morning activities, integrating some variety, so you can be ready to greet your students—which is a great way to start the day. (See also the tip on page 34.)

Bathroom Sign-Out/Sign-In Place this form on a clipboard near the door. Attach a pencil to the clipboard so students don't have to spend time finding one. If there is not a clock close by, or you're working with young students who may not yet know how to tell time, place a small digital clock near the sheet. As with any other routine, you will need to practice this one with students. Model how to get permission to use the bathroom, how to put the tennis ball container or other object (to show who's out of the room) on their desk, and how to sign out and in.

Homework Guidelines Once you have developed your homework routines, make sure you share them with students and parents. This handout, addressed to parents, is designed to help you communicate your reasons for doing homework, the types of homework that parents can expect to see, and the homework schedule. You can also include consequences for not turning in homework on time.

Homework Tips Include these tips in your Back to School Night/Curriculum Night packet and/or hand them out at parent conferences. Homework is designed to teach students to be responsible, but they need their parents to help them establish effective homework routines at home.

Homework Contracts for Grades K–5 Samples of contracts for each grade are shown. The contracts are designed to remind families about the purposes of homework, the types of homework they should expect to see, the grade-level homework expectations, and the homework schedule. These contracts offer a variety of ideas, so you can tailor them to the needs of your students. Be mindful of the general rule of 10 minutes of homework for each grade level when you draw up the homework contracts.

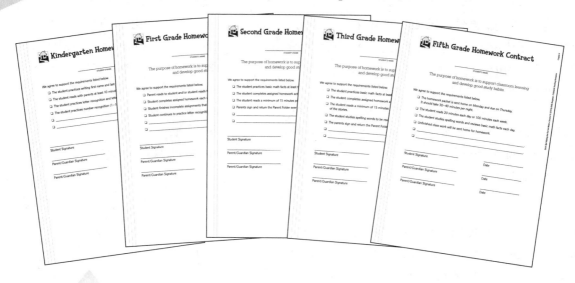

Kelly's Tip

To make sure that you provide a wide variety of morning activities, you might create a daily schedule. For instance, Monday might be your linguistic day, when students respond to or write a poem, an advertisement, or a comic strip. Tuesday might be your logical/mathematical day, when students create or complete a chart, crossword puzzle, or graph.

Take Action ·············

- Develop an arrival routine for students—decide which tasks need to be done, what morning activities will look like, and which notebook will be used for morning activities.

- Develop the dismissal routine—decide which tasks need to be done before students leave each day. Is it possible to get the tasks done and read aloud to students for the last few minutes of the day?

- Establish your bathroom procedures—decide when students will be able to use the bathroom. How will they get your permission to do so? How will you know who is out of the room?

- Design your homework routines and policies—decide what kinds of homework will be sent home and create a schedule. Will there be a regular homework schedule or as needed? How much reading should students be doing at home?

Morning Activities

Morning activities are designed to get students engaged in learning as soon as they walk into the classroom. To encourage students to settle down quickly and focus on the task, you might have classical music playing. Definitely have an activity written on the board or displayed onscreen so students can start learning immediately. Some morning activities can be done in student journals, while others might need special materials. If special materials are needed, remember to place them on students' desks before they arrive.

Here are ideas and tools for planning your morning activities.

Morning Activities for Grades K–2

❑ Edit sentences and/or paragraphs to practice proofreading and editing.

- Give each student a copy of a short sentence and have him or her correct capital letters and punctuation.

- Write a sentence on the board or display it on a screen and ask students to copy it correctly.

- Give each student a copy of a sentence, write it on the board, or display it on a screen, and have everyone correct a frequently used word that is misspelled.

❑ Solve math problems.

- Give two or three simple math problems to be solved. At the kindergarten level, you might provide manipulatives for students to use.

- Ask students to list or draw pictures of things that are circles or another shape.

- If you've been practicing using tally marks, give students two or three numbers and ask them to write tally marks for those numbers.

❑ Respond to your current read-aloud book.

- Ask students to draw a picture of the setting of the story.

- Have students draw a picture of the main character of the story.

- Tell students to write a different ending for the story.

❑ Review content.

- Ask students to write words or draw pictures to summarize what they've learned about a topic you're studying.

- Have students tell a partner everything they've learned about a topic you're studying.

Morning Activities

Morning Activities for Grades 3–5

- ❏ Edit sentences and/or paragraphs to practice proofreading and editing.

- ❏ Solve math problems.

- ❏ Respond to a current read-aloud book.

- ❏ Respond to an inspiring, character-building quote (see below).

- ❏ Choose a short activity from the Multiple Intelligences Activities page. Examples:

  - • Write a poem about a place you'd like to visit. (Linguistic Intelligence)
  - • Make a crossword puzzle using words from a hobby you have. (Logical/Mathematical Intelligence)
  - • Draw a bulletin board for a movie you've seen. (Spatial Intelligence)

Quotes

Kind words can be short and easy to speak, but their echoes are truly endless. —*Mother Teresa*

Man's mind, once stretched by a new idea, never regains its original dimension. —*Oliver Wendell Holmes*

Take time to read . . . it is the fountain of wisdom. —*Unknown*

Knowledge becomes wisdom only after it has been put to practical use. —*Unknown*

Excellence is never an accident. —*Albert Einstein*

Most smiles start with another smile. —*Unknown*

Learn from the mistakes made by others. You won't live long enough to make them all yourself. —*Unknown*

A kindness done today is the surest way to a brighter tomorrow. —*Unknown*

The smallest act of kindness is worth more than the grandest intention. —*Oscar Wilde*

When someone does something good, applaud! You will make two people happy. —*Samuel Goldwyn*

Cheerfulness is the atmosphere in which all things thrive. —*Jean Paul Richter*

There are many different languages but a smile speaks for all of them. —*No Bullying Program*

Every job is a self-portrait of the person who did it. Autograph your work with excellence. —*Jessica Guidobono*

Problems are opportunities to participate in life. —*Unknown*

In the race to success, there is no finish line. —*Mike Shanahan*

Success comes in cans, not in cannots. —*John Ralston*

Be more positive than any of your friends, family, or co-workers. —*Mike Shanahan*

If you solve the little problems on a daily basis, very seldom do you encounter the big problems. —*Mike Shanahan*

Multiple Intelligences Activities

1. Select an area of intelligence and product from the following list:

LINGUISTIC
Poem
Pamphlet
Advertisement
Comic Strip

LOGICAL/MATHEMATICAL
Riddle
Chart
Crossword Puzzle
Graph

SPATIAL
Bulletin Board
Collage
Flipbook
Story Cube

BODILY-KINESTHETIC
Role Play
Pantomime
Dance
Food

MUSICAL
Song
List Sounds
Choral Reading
Rap Song

INTERPERSONAL
Press Conference
Demonstration
TV Program
Fairy Tale

INTRAPERSONAL
Diary
Timeline
Family Tree
Journal

2. Choose one of the following prompts for the product you chose in step 1:

- ❏ Describe your pet or a pet you wish you had.
- ❏ Write about a trip you'd like to take.
- ❏ What is a game you like to play?
- ❏ Tell about a hobby you have.
- ❏ Describe your best day at school.
- ❏ It's raining cats and dogs. What do you do?
- ❏ Name places where you can go barefoot.
- ❏ List possible uses of a paintbrush.
- ❏ If coins could no longer be spent, what could they be used for?
- ❏ You just developed a plan to get rich quick. What is it?
- ❏ You can take only one picture for a contest. What would you photograph?
- ❏ Design your ideal miniature golf course.
- ❏ Design a hot air balloon and explain what it represents.
- ❏ If your house were a boat, how would life be different?
- ❏ You have been invited on a space shuttle ride and a walk on the moon. Name one thing you would take and explain why.
- ❏ It was only an empty box, but . . .
- ❏ When I heard the bell, I knew . . .
- ❏ When she opened the envelope . . .
- ❏ Name things that plug in.
- ❏ Name things that are a challenge.
- ❏ Name good ways to remember something important.
- ❏ If you were a food, what would you be? Why?
- ❏ What if apples were as large as basketballs?
- ❏ Name foods that are round.
- ❏ Combine two foods and invent a name for this combination.
- ❏ Name different types of candy.
- ❏ Name something you can use in place of a sled.
- ❏ If I met the president, then . . .
- ❏ If I could be a parent for one day, then . . .
- ❏ If I could be one inch tall, then . . .
- ❏ If I could become invisible, then . . .
- ❏ If I were locked in a toy store all night, then . . .
- ❏ What would you substitute if there were no chairs?
- ❏ Name an interesting job to have.
- ❏ Make up a new flavor of jelly bean.
- ❏ It's your lucky day. What might happen?
- ❏ If a toothbrush could talk, what would it say?
- ❏ If a shoe could talk, what would it say?

 # Homework Tips

How should we set up a homework schedule at home?

Schedule a regular homework time for the same time each night. Look at your family calendar for the week and schedule homework around other events. For instance, if baseball practice is on Monday, Wednesday, and Thursday from 6:00 p.m. to 7:30 p.m., you probably want to schedule homework time before baseball on those days. You might consider posting a calendar or a sign in your kitchen that shows what time your child should be doing homework so that everyone is clear about the time—and you can support your child.

How long should homework take?

Parents often wonder how much time their children should spend on homework each evening. The general rule of thumb is 10 minutes for each grade in school. That means 10 minutes in first grade, 20 minutes in second grade, 30 minutes in third grade, and so on. Set a timer for each child so you can keep track of everyone's time.

What if my child doesn't have any homework?

Have your child do something school-related for the amount of time normally scheduled for homework. For instance, he or she can make up math problems and solve them, read, do research, practice spelling, or practice math facts. Some parents purchase workbooks for their children to work on if they don't have homework. Having students do some sort of school-related work every school night will encourage them to get their homework done. They will be less likely to "forget" that they have homework if they know they're going to have homework time anyway.

How do we set up a homework space in our home?

Each child should have a special place for homework. This could be a bedroom desk or a kitchen table. Wherever you set up the space, have in place all the supplies your child will need so you don't spend valuable time searching for them. The study place should be quiet or have soft instrumental music playing so your child can concentrate. Turn down the TV—or turn it off—and avoid other sounds that may be distracting.

How much should I help my child with homework?

Parents often wonder how much they should help with homework. There isn't a clear-cut answer. The answer falls somewhere between none at all and doing the assignment for your child. As a parent, you need to discover your child's frustration level in each subject area and then help with the homework right before he or she reaches that level. Your child may do really well in reading but may struggle with math. In this case, you may want to have your child simply check in with you after completing a reading assignment. However, you may need to guide him or her through the directions for a math assignment and go over at least one example to ensure he or she remains focused and feels capable. Try asking questions about the work your child has done and more guided questions to get him or her headed in the right direction. Never do a homework assignment for your child—he or she will miss the entire learning opportunity.

Chapter 5

Get to Know Your Students

Scenario A It's the day before school starts, and your school has planned an Open House for students to visit the classroom, bring their school supplies, and meet their teachers. You're a nervous wreck about meeting students and parents for the first time, and you just want the Open House to be over. You know you're supposed to learn as much as you can about your students, but you have no idea how to do this. This morning you found out that you'll have five students who are on IEPs, and you're wondering how you'll keep track of all of their goals. How will you survive?

Scenario B Your school's Open House is this afternoon, and you're excited to meet the families. You have activities planned for parents and students to do while they wait their turn to meet you. After the Open House today, you'll have some great information about your students so that you'll know a little bit about them when school starts tomorrow. You have a plan in mind for your students on IEPs, and you're really ready to get the kids in the door so you can start teaching. You can't wait to get to know your students!

First impressions are very important, especially if you're a new teacher or new to a school. An Open House is a time when families can come and go as they please. You'll probably have many families arrive at the same time, and they'll all be eager to meet you. Be prepared for your Open House and make a great first impression!

Tips for Success • • • • • • • • • •

Meet Your Students and Their Parents for the First Time Many schools have some sort of Open House or Meet-and-Greet before school starts. This is a great time to learn as much as you can about your students so you can hit the ground running when they arrive on the first day of school. Here are some things you can do to make this event a success:

■ *When Families Arrive*: Have a note on the board that looks something like this:

> Welcome!
>
> Please add your name to the list on the other side of the board. This will help me to make sure I meet each family in the order in which you arrive.
>
> Students, please select one of the numbers from the board. Find the matching number on one of the desks to find the spot where you'll sit on the first day of school.
>
> On that desk, you will find a list of activities to complete while you're here.
>
> I'm looking forward to working with you this year!

■ *While Families Are in Your Classroom*: Place the Open House Activity Checklist for Students on each desk to tell students and parents what to do while they're in your classroom. Most students will bring their school supplies, so you'll want to make sure students know what to do with them. This is the perfect time to get information from students and parents. Ask parents to complete the Student Information Card while students complete the Student Interest Survey. Then encourage students and parents to explore the classroom with a Classroom Scavenger Hunt.

Kelly's Tip

Some parents may want to use the Open House as a time to hold a conference with you. Because you will have many families waiting to meet you, make sure you have a way to politely tell those parents that you are not able to have lengthy conversations, but that you will be happy to follow up with them. Make copies of the Open House Parent Note to Teacher so that parents can write down the information for you or ask you to contact them. Remember, this is your first impression, so you want to be responsive to each parent while making sure that you give ample time to all families.

Organize Important Student Information The more you know about your students, the better you will be able to work with them. After you've met your students, be sure to review these important pieces of information.

- *Health Issues:* The first, and most important, information you want to collect is about any health issues. Check with your school nurse, clinic aide, or office staff to find out if any of your students have health issues. Make sure you have copies of their written health plans and review those carefully. Keep two copies of the health plans, one in your Substitute Teacher Folder (see Chapter 8), and one in a safe place, such as a clipboard or each student's individual file (see Chapter 2).

- *Learning Plans:* Students will come to you with a variety of different learning plans including special education plans, 504 plans, advanced learning plans, reading plans, behavior plans, and so on. Use the Learning Plan Goal Sheet to compile the information from these plans so you can review it frequently.

Kelly's Tip

Use a clipboard to keep important information in one, easily accessible location. Place copies of student health plans on the clipboard. After completing the Learning Plan Goal Sheet, keep copies of it on the clipboard. If you're collecting money for a field trip, put the checklist on the clipboard. By doing this, you know that all of your important information is at your fingertips and you don't have to spend time searching for it.

Use What You Know About Your Students to Plan Your Instruction Now that you have all of your important student information organized, use it to design your instruction to meet the needs of all your students. Each time you do your planning, refer back to the Learning Plan Goal Sheet to make sure that you are addressing individual student goals. If you are planning an activity that involves food, refer to the health plans to make sure that there will be no issues for your students. Gathering the information is an important first step but using it for your instruction is even more important.

TOOLS FOR SUCCESS

There is a lot to learn about your students! The more you know, the more effective you can be as a teacher. The following templates will help you get to know your students and organize the information that you collect. Each of the following templates appears on the CD (see CD, Chapter 5 folder).

Open House Teacher Checklist
Use this checklist to prepare for the first meeting with your students and their families. Make a great first impression by being prepared and organized when they arrive in your classroom. You can record your thoughts in the spaces provided on the checklist template.

Open House Activity
Place this checklist on each student desk for families to complete when they come to the Open House. This checklist will give them things to do while you meet with other families. It will also show that you are fully capable of having several things going on in your classroom at one time.

Open House Parent Note to Teacher
Almost certainly you will have one or more parents who want to have a conference with you during Open House. Give them this short form to complete so you can get the information you need and/or follow up with parents.

Student Information Card
Parents/guardians complete information cards for the office, but it's nice for you to have your own set of information. Ask parents/guardians to complete this form so you have current, accurate information for each student. The template shows blanks for parents, but you can modify the form on the CD for those students who have guardians.

Student Interest Survey

Get to know your students by finding out what they're interested in. Whenever possible, use their interests to connect with them. Perhaps one of your students has the same hobby as you do. If you take a couple of minutes to discuss this hobby with the student, you will have an immediate connection. Perhaps another student has an interest in a topic that you know nothing about. Ask this student to teach you a little bit about the hobby, and you'll develop a bond. Whenever possible, integrate students' interests into your instruction to make the learning more meaningful.

Classroom Scavenger Hunt

Encourage students and parents to explore the classroom and then have them complete the Scavenger Hunt sheet.

Learning Plan Goal Sheet

Use this form to compile all the information from your individual student learning plans. Keep a copy of it in a convenient place, such as your clipboard, to use when planning and/or preparing for parent conferences. If you decide you want to have this information in front of you at the conferences, make a copy of the sheet and cut apart the sections for each student. For confidentiality reasons, you won't want to have a Learning Plan Goal Sheet with information on several students in sight of parents.

Take Action • • • • • • • • • • • • •

- ■ Prepare for your first meeting with students and parents.
- ■ Check to see if any of your students have health issues.
- ■ Find out if any of your students have learning plans.
- ■ Organize important information about your students.

Chapter 6

Have a Successful First Week of School

Scenario A You spend the entire first day of school telling students what the rules and routines are. Since you've covered everything, you expect students to follow all of the rules immediately. However, students look like they're drifting between sleep and fear. They're not only tired of listening to you talk, but they're also afraid of missing anything. At the end of the first day, you feel exhausted because you've talked "at" the students all day long and you didn't have much fun. You made it through the first day, but what will you do with the rest of the week?

Scenario B As soon as the bell rings on the first day of school, you immediately engage students in a high-interest activity that is part of your curriculum. At one point during the day, you play a name game and practice a couple of your classroom policies. Each day of the first week of school will look something like this. By the end of the week, students will have participated in fun learning activities, so they know that it's going to be a great year. They will have practiced all of the classroom routines, so they understand those routines. You're excited about the second week of school because you can delve into your regular daily schedule.

The first week of school is a time to review classroom expectations, but it's also a time to get students engaged in learning. You want them to be excited about being in your classroom. Make sure that the first week of school includes a nice balance of fun learning, name games, and sharing classroom expectations.

Tips for Success • • • • • • • • •

Get Students Engaged in Learning Review the social studies and science units for the year. Work with your teammates to decide if there is one unit that is especially high-interest and would be a good one to start off the school year. Once you've chosen the unit, develop some activities that will engage students in their learning while working with each other. Plan at least one activity for each day of the first week of school.

Plan for the First Week of School How can you involve students in fun learning activities beginning on the first day of school? If your goal is to create a warm, caring learning environment, starting with classroom rules the morning of the first day of school will defeat that purpose. Instead, begin with one of your social studies or science units that is high-interest and gets students involved in learning right away. Other activities for the first week of school should include the following:

- *Learning Students' Names*: Plan an activity each day to practice students' names. Obviously, it's important for you to learn student names quickly, but it's also important for students to learn one another's names.

- *Practicing Classroom Routines*: Have some fun with this task. Demonstrate what it should look like when students arrive in the morning, then have them load up their backpacks, leave the classroom, and enter again to practice what you demonstrated. Use the same process when you want students to practice lining up for recess. Also, after asking students to talk to their neighbors, rehearse your signal for getting their attention. Make it a challenge to see how quickly they can do this by using a stopwatch. This is a fun way to reinforce speed and refocusing.

- *Organizing Supplies*: Review the list of supplies that students will be bringing (Chapter 1) and make sure you have a plan for each item. Spend a little time each day organizing these supplies. If the supplies are community supplies, such as tissues and copy paper, put them in specific areas and arrange them by importance and accessibility to you and students. If the supplies are individual supplies, allow time for students to put their names on each item and label it appropriately or provide preprinted labels. For instance, if students are expected to bring four spiral notebooks, one might be labeled "Writer's Notebook" and one might be labeled "Morning Work." You'll want to have permanent markers available for this task.

- *Reviewing Classroom Rules*: If students are going to help establish your classroom rules, plan a time and a procedure for doing this. Will they work in small groups? Who will make the final decisions? Who will make the classroom display of rules? Once the rules are established, have fun practicing them. Ask students to act out examples of following the rules and breaking them. For example, you might ask: What does it look like when you are not treating each other well? Why is it helpful to have this rule?

- *Touring the School*: Depending on the grade level you teach and/or the number of new students in your class, you may want to take a tour of the school. You can also have some fun with this by doing a scavenger hunt.

- *Taking a Picture of Each Student*: You will find that these pictures are invaluable! If you are a person who has a hard time remembering names, use the photos to make a class seating chart so you can learn names more quickly. This seating chart will also be very helpful for substitute teachers. You may also use these photos for all-about-me activities to begin the year, as well as other activities during the school year.

Review Classroom Expectations Decide which routines you want to review with students the first week of school and develop ways to practice these routines. Again, have fun with this practice. For instance, one of your classroom rules probably has to do with taking care of supplies. When reviewing the classroom rules, ask students to act out good and bad examples of taking care of supplies. You will also want to practice your arrival routines (see Chapter 4). When doing this, have students practice by acting out the wrong way to do a routine and the right way to do it. Not only will they have more fun, but they will also clearly remember the difference between the two activities.

TOOLS FOR SUCCESS

The first week of school sets the tone for the rest of the school year. You will want to make sure that students are engaged in fun learning activities while you also make time to review classroom procedures. Each of the following templates appears in the CD (see CD, Chapter 6 folder).

First Week Planning Tools: There are many, many things to think about regarding the first week of school, but a few rise to the top: supplies, learning names, engaging students in learning, and classroom routines. Students will be bringing in lots of supplies when they come to school for the first time. You'll need to determine a purpose for each supply, and this template helps you do that. One of the most important things to do once students arrive is to learn their names. Use the space in this template to list some name games that will help you learn student names and help students learn each other's names. You want your first week of school to be fun and engaging so it sets the tone for the rest of the year. This template will also aid you in choosing a high-interest curriculum unit to get students learning right away. Finally, you will need to spend some time each day during the first week of school practicing rules and routines. Decide which routines you'll practice each day and record them on the template. A completed sample is shown on the next page.

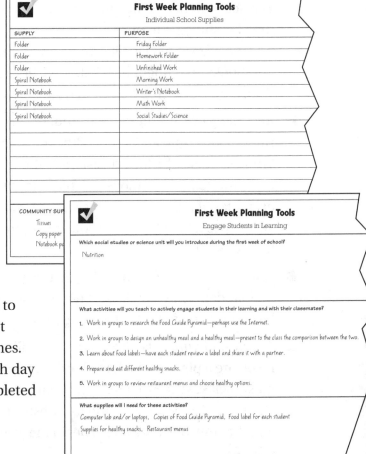

First Week Planning Tools

Planning Grid

	DAY 1	DAY 2	DAY 3	DAY 4	DAY 5
NAME GAMES	Each student draws picture of something important to him/her. Throughout day, students introduce themselves to class and share their pictures.	Assign a partner to each student and give each pair five interview questions. Each student will introduce his/her partner to rest of class and share answers to three of the five questions.	Ball Toss: Class stands in circle. Teacher tosses ball to a student while saying student's name. Students toss ball to other students who haven't caught it yet. Class can help with names.	Each student receives a card with another student's name on it. They pair up with that student, find one thing they have in common, and share it with class.	Ask for a student volunteer to go around the room and name every student. Have students move to different desks and ask for another student volunteer. Repeat several times.
LEARNING ACTIVITIES	Research Food Guide Pyramid	Design a healthy meal and an unhealthy meal	Learn about food labels	Prepare healthy snacks	Review restaurant menus
CLASSROOM PROCEDURES	Practice dismissal routine Review arrival routine & practice it tomorrow	Practice arrival routine	Practice lining up to leave the room	Practice lining up to come in from recess	Practice classroom rules

Quick Tips! Making the First Six Weeks a Success! © 2010 by Kelly Bergman • Scholastic Teaching Resources. Chapter 6

School Tour Scavenger Hunt Make sure that students know all of the important places in the building. Give students clipboards (or have them use folders), take them on a tour of the school, and have them complete this sheet on the scavenger hunt.

Take Action ••••••••••••

- Review supply lists and decide which items will be community supplies and which will be individual supplies. Choose labels for individual supplies. Print labels if you decide to use this strategy.

- Select a curriculum unit that is high-interest and can involve students immediately in learning and working with others.

- Decide how you will review and practice classroom routines.

- Begin learning students' names as soon as they arrive. Not only do you need to learn all of their names, but they also need to learn the names of their classmates.

Chapter 7

Begin to Develop Lasting Relationships With Parents

Scenario A Back to School Night/Curriculum Night is tonight. This is your chance to make a great impression on parents, but you're not sure where to begin. You know that you should talk a bit about the curriculum, a bit about field trips, and probably a bit about parent volunteers. Oh, no! You haven't even thought much about parent volunteers so you'll have to try to do that another time. How are you going to pull this all together in the next few hours?

Scenario B Back to School Night/Curriculum Night is tonight. This is your chance to make a great impression on parents, and you're well prepared. Your agenda and materials are ready; you just need to add some finishing touches. You've also solidified your plans for making the best use of parent volunteers, and you're excited about getting them started in the classroom. In just a few more hours, you'll be able to make a great first impression!

Back to School Night/Curriculum Night is an important time to begin establishing relationships with parents. They come to this event to find out what their children will be learning during the year and to find out about important policies and procedures. Being prepared for this event will help lay a strong foundation for working with parents the rest of the school year. After Back to School Night/Curriculum Night, you can begin your work with parent volunteers because they have a better understanding of your classroom.

Tips for Success • • • • • • • • • •

Plan Your Back to School Night/Curriculum Night Agenda If your teammates have indicated that you're responsible for doing your own Back to School Night/Curriculum Night, your next step is to plan your agenda. Here are some important items to consider including in it:

- *Daily Schedule*: You probably have this posted in your classroom, and you'll want to take a couple of minutes to review it with parents so they can get a feel for a typical day in the classroom. Parents may also like to have a copy to take home.

- *Curriculum*: Parents want to have a general idea of what instruction will look like in your classroom. You don't want to overwhelm them with information, but a brief overview is helpful. To describe what reading instruction will look like in your classroom, for instance, you might describe what a reading group looks like and what the other students are doing while you meet with the group. Think about providing a brief written summary of your curriculum.

- *Homework*: Parents are always anxious to know what they can expect for homework. What are the homework policies for your classroom? What will students be expected to do each night/each week? How much should families be reading at home? Have a copy of Homework Tips to give to parents so they know what to expect. (See Chapter 4, page 38.)

- *Field Trips*: Parents also want to know about any field trips you've scheduled during the year. Have the dates available and be prepared to tell parents how they can volunteer to help.

- *Parent Volunteers*: Some parents will ask how and when can they volunteer in the classroom. (See more in the sections below.)

- *Communicating With You*: Aside from instruction, parent communication is one of the most important aspects of your job. What is the best way for parents to communicate with you (e-mail or voice mail)? If they send you an e-mail message or leave you a voice-mail message, about how long will it take you to get back to them? How will you communicate with them? Will you send weekly (or monthly) newsletters?

Kelly's Tip

Take pictures during different subjects and activities throughout the school year to show what goes on in your classroom during the day. Make sure that you have pictures of activities for each of the content areas. Upload these pictures into a file called "Back to School Night/Curriculum Night" and use them next year during your Back to School Night/Curriculum Night presentation. Prepare a slide show so that parents can see the activities while you're talking about them. This also helps take some of the pressure off of you because parents will be looking at the slides instead of staring at you the whole time.

Put Together a Packet of Handouts for Back to School Night/ Curriculum Night This packet should include a copy of the daily schedule, some highlights of the curriculum (What will students be working on in reading, writing, math, social studies, and science this year?), and copies of the homework policy. Your contact information should be placed on the front of the packet. Make about five extra copies of this packet and place them in your Back to School Night/ Curriculum Night file (see Chapter 2) to give to new students who arrive in your classroom during the school year.

Tip Write students' names on the front of the packets of handouts and place them on their desks. When parents arrive, ask them to pick up the handouts from their child's desk. At the end of the night, you will have a quick review of which parents were able to attend and which were not. Send the packets home with those students whose parents were not able to attend the event. Consider taking one extra step by placing a phone call to those parents to let them know that the packets are being sent home and that they can contact you with any questions.

Plan for Parent Volunteers The following questions are some of those included in the Parent Volunteer Planning Sheet on the CD and will help you solidify your thinking about the use of parent volunteers in your classroom.

■ *How often will you have parent volunteers in your classroom?* Some teachers like to have parent volunteers every day of the week. Other teachers think that Mondays and Fridays can be more hectic than other days so they don't have parent volunteers on those days. Some teachers have their library day scheduled on Tuesday and won't be doing small group reading instruction that day so they don't have parent volunteers then. Think carefully about your daily and weekly schedules to decide which days of the week you'll ask for volunteers. Also consider whether certain times of the day are more suitable for volunteers.

■ *How will you schedule your parent volunteers?* One possibility is to have a blank calendar (similar to the one on the next page) available at Back to School Night/ Curriculum Night and ask parents to sign up for the days that work best for them. Then, at the end of each month, you can transfer this information to the calendar for the upcoming month, make enough copies for your volunteers, highlight each volunteer's times on the calendar, and send the calendars home with students. This way, there are no surprises; parents have tentatively marked these days on their calendars, and the dates are confirmed when they receive your calendar.

Another option is to ask parents on which days of the week they are and are not available. You can then transfer this information to a master calendar. At the end of each month, sit down with your master calendar and the calendar for the upcoming month to assign parent volunteers. Again, make

Tip After the first two months of school, you will know your paraprofessional/aide and parent volunteers fairly well. You may decide that you can turn over the task of drawing up the volunteer calendar to one of these trusted people. It's one fewer thing you will have to be responsible for.

enough copies for the volunteers, highlight each person's name on one calendar, and send calendars home with students.

Monthly Calendar				
Volunteer Schedule				
1ST MONDAY	1ST TUESDAY	1ST WEDNESDAY	1ST THURSDAY	1ST FRIDAY
2ND MONDAY	2ND TUESDAY	2ND WEDNESDAY	2ND THURSDAY	2ND FRIDAY
3RD MONDAY	3RD TUESDAY	3RD WEDNESDAY	3RD THURSDAY	3RD FRIDAY

■ *What will parents do when they're in your classroom?* How much time will parents spend on clerical work? How much time will they spend working with children? Will they work with individual students, small groups, or the whole class? Once you know your parent volunteers, you may feel comfortable having them monitor the large group of students when you spend more focused time working with small groups.

Here's an example of a parent volunteer routine in one classroom: As the students are taking care of their arrival "chores," the teacher greets the volunteer and explains the clerical work that needs to be done. The parent works on that while the class does its opening activities. When it's time for small groups to meet, the teacher works with one group, the volunteer works with one group, the paraprofessional/aide works with one group, and one group works independently. The teacher may do more than one rotation each day, so the volunteer may work with two groups.

Kelly's Tip Keep a basket in your classroom labeled "Clerical Work for Parent Volunteers." When parents have time to do clerical work (cutting, putting things together, grading, etc.), they can go to the basket and find projects to work on. The earlier you can plan, the easier it will be to have parents prepare materials for upcoming projects. You might even consider putting the date of the project on top of the materials, so that parents will know when that project needs to be done.

■ *How will you communicate your expectations to parent volunteers?* All parents want the best for their children. Some parents volunteer in the classroom to help the teacher, some volunteer to see what goes on in the classroom, some volunteer because they want extra time to be with their children, and some volunteer for a combination of these reasons or for completely different reasons. Some parents have volunteered before, and others have not. Parents need to know that professionalism and confidentiality are extremely important in the classroom. You will need to be sure to communicate very clear expectations to your parent volunteers. It would be ideal to have some type of parent volunteer training session, but it can be difficult to get all your volunteers in one place, at one time. The next best thing is to give them a copy of the Parent Volunteer Tips reproducible and ask them to sign it to confirm that they've read the information.

Collect Scheduling Information for Parent Conferences If you want to think as far ahead as parent conferences, Back to School Night/Curriculum Night is the time to ask parents about their scheduling preferences. Set out the Parent Conference Preliminary Scheduling Form (see the CD) so that parents can tell you when they're available for conferences.

TOOLS FOR SUCCESS

Working with parents is a very important part of teaching. It's crucial to begin developing positive relationships with them at the beginning of the year. These tools will help you build and foster outstanding relationships with parents. Each of the following templates appears on the CD (see CD, Chapter 7 folder).

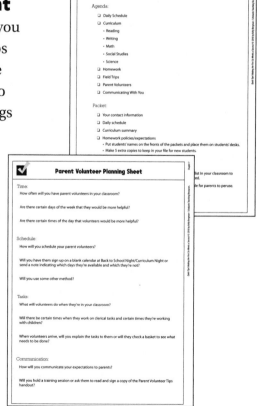

Back to School Night/Curriculum Night Planning Sheet Use this template to help you

prepare for this special evening. The first section helps you plan your agenda. The second section gives some ideas for handouts to include in the packet you give to parents. The last section offers ideas about other things to have ready for the evening.

Parent Volunteer Planning Sheet

Use this sheet to decide how you will use parent volunteers in your classroom.

Parent Volunteer Form and Monthly Calendar Some volunteers are very comfortable working with students; others are not. Some are comfortable doing clerical work; others are not. With this form, collect contact information from your volunteers and find out what they're comfortable doing when they're in the classroom. If you find out that a parent is not comfortable working with children, you may want to schedule that person during social studies and science time rather than reading time, when you want as many adults as possible working with small groups. Conversely, if you find out that you have a parent who is not comfortable doing clerical work, schedule that person at a time when they can work with students.

Parent Volunteer Tips You need to be very clear about your expectations for classroom volunteers. They need to know that they must be professional and must maintain confidentiality. Use this handout to communicate your expectations to your volunteers.

Parent Conference Preliminary Scheduling Form Although Back to School Night/Curriculum Night is too early for most people to schedule specific times for conferences, this is a good time to find out what times work best for families. Use this form to record parents' availability for conferences. Place the completed forms in your "Parent Conferences" file (see Chapter 2).

Take Action

- Use the Back to School Night/Curriculum Night Planning Sheet to prepare for this important event.

- Use the Parent Volunteer Planning Sheet to make decisions about the role of volunteers in your classroom.

- Schedule your first round of volunteers and communicate your expectations to them.

Chapter 8

Prepare for Substitute Teachers So Learning Continues While You're Away

Scenario A It's the third week of school, and you wake up with a horrible sore throat. You've worked so hard these last couple of weeks, and it's finally caught up to you. There is no way you can teach today, but you are not at all prepared to have a substitute in your classroom. You know that you'll return to chaos unless you drag yourself out of bed, drive to school, and write detailed plans for your substitute teacher. You think: *I really am responsible for these students, even if I can't be there to teach them!*

Scenario B It's the third week of school, and you wake up with a horrible sore throat. You've worked so hard these last couple of weeks, and it's finally caught up to you. You take a deep breath and think: *Everything is going to be okay.* Your Substitute Folder is ready, your plans are written in your plan book (you can ask the substitute to call you for additional details), and you have a box on the back shelf with all of today's materials in it. You think: *I am responsible for these students and they should be able to carry on without me. Thank goodness I took the time to prepare for a situation just like this!*

There is nothing worse than waking up sick one morning and feeling like you have to get to school to prepare for a substitute. Your brain is not working at full speed, and you can't remember all the important details that you need to tell a substitute. Save yourself this agony by preparing ahead of time. Your class can run smoothly, and the learning can continue while you're gone.

Tips for Success • • • • • • • • •

Prepare for a Substitute Teacher Long Before You Need One

Teachers sometimes believe that there is no one who can replace them. The only way to feel comfortable having someone else in your classroom is to make sure that you are well prepared. Make sure that your substitute has all the vital information he or she needs so that learning can continue while you're away.

Kelly's Tip *Try using the term "guest teacher." It's a nicer phrase than "substitute teacher" and may help your students show more respect.*

TOOLS FOR SUCCESS

There are so many things to think about in managing a classroom—it's difficult to remember all the little details that have become natural to you. It's important to get every one of those details written out so that a guest teacher can step into your classroom and keep the learning going while you're out. These tools will help you plan and organize for that day when you have to be away from the classroom. Each of the following templates appears on the CD (see CD folder, Chapter 8).

✔ **Guest Teacher Information Form** Use this comprehensive template to make sure that your guest teacher has everything he or she needs to provide continuity in students' learning. After writing your name at the top of the form, fill in the rest of form; pay special attention to these sections:

■ *Students With Health Issues/Allergies*: It is your responsibility to make sure that this important (and highly confidential) information is communicated to anyone left in charge of your class. Take this section very seriously, so there are no mistakes.

■ *Legal or Custody Issues*: As with the previous section, it is critical that this information is communicated to guest teachers. These considerations have been placed at the top of the template because they are such significant safety issues.

■ *Students With Other Needs/ Strategies That Work With Them*: Teachers have a true talent for finding strategies that work with their students. Be sure to share these with guest teachers so they can be as efficient working with those students as you are.

- *Students Who Attend Special Classes: When/Where*: Make sure that your guest teacher will be in complete control of the classroom by informing him or her about students who attend other classes, the times they leave, and where they go.

- *Computer Codes/Passwords:* Guest teachers will likely need the computers, whether it's for attendance or student work, and you want to be sure they have the appropriate access codes.

- *Parent Volunteers*: In Chapter 7, I discussed scheduling parent volunteers, giving them tips about working in the classroom, and having a place for them to get their work. Place a copy of your Parent Volunteer Calendar in the Guest Teacher folder each month so that the substitute will know whether or not a parent volunteer is coming in. Place a copy of your Parent Volunteer Tips in the folder also, so that the guest teacher knows what to expect from the volunteer.

Take Action • • • • • • • • • • • •

- Fill in the appropriate pieces of information in the Guest Teacher Information Form.

- Gather the appropriate materials to file in the Guest Teacher folder.

- Keep the Guest Teacher folder in a place that is easily accessible.

- Update the folder as necessary: replace the class list when you get a new student, update health plans as you need to, and so forth.

Chapter 9

Build on the Relationships You've Developed With Parents

Scenario A School has gotten off to a good start. You feel great about the routines you've established with your students, and you're proud of the work your students are doing. Today, you check your voice mail during your planning period and find a very angry message from one student's mother saying that she has no idea what's going on in the classroom. She wants to know what her child is learning about in school. Because this is your first parent concern, you have no idea what to say when you return the call. You wait a couple of days trying to figure out what to say and, by the time you finally return the call, the mother is absolutely furious. How can you possibly make this situation better?

Scenario B School has gotten off to a good start. You feel great about the routines you've established with your students, and you're proud of the work they are doing. You've sent home your first classroom newsletter and kept parents well informed about the learning that is taking place in your classroom. Today, you check your voice mail during your planning period and find a nice message from a parent thanking you for being so good about communicating with parents. She appreciates the time you take to make phone calls and send home the classroom newsletter. You're now much more confident about the relationships you have with your classroom parents.

Communicating with parents can be easy, and they really appreciate it. Keeping lines of communication open will allow you to work closely with parents and avoid conflicts. There may still be an occasional conflict, but it will be much easier to handle if you've been proactive with your parent relationships. Some of your communication will be done in person, some over the telephone, and some via e-mail. In the following sections, "talk" may be talking by e-mail. Regardless of how you communicate with parents, the same guidelines apply.

Tips for Success · · · · · · · · · · ·

Communicate Well With Parents Parents like to know what's going on in their child's classroom. The easiest way to keep them informed is to send a monthly newsletter home with students. Tell parents what their children are learning so they can support that learning at home.

Kelly's
Tip Make sure that your communication with parents is professional and timely. Ask at least one person to proofread every document that you send home to parents. In addition, make sure that you give parents plenty of advance notice about upcoming events. Field trip notes should be sent home at least three weeks in advance so that parents have time to respond and make appropriate arrangements.

Handle Parent Concerns Effectively You've done your best to communicate with parents, but a conflict has arisen. Following these four steps will help you solve almost every problem.

- **Step 1:** *Listen* When parents know that you have truly heard and understood their concern, they will be more likely to work with you to resolve the conflict. Listen carefully to the concern without interrupting. Take notes if you need to.

- **Step 2:** *Summarize* The best way to show parents that you have listened to their concern is to briefly summarize what you heard. Take a moment to tell them what you have heard and make sure you're both talking about the same issue before attempting to develop a resolution.

- **Step 3:** *Respond* Once both parties agree on the issue, it is time for you to respond. Sometimes there is a quick fix, and you can take care of it right then. Other times you may have to do some research to get to the bottom of the issue. It is fine to tell parents that you will check into the issue and get back to them. Be sure to tell parents when you'll get back to them and then be sure you do so.

- **Step 4:** *Follow-up* Following up might mean calling parents back after you've told them that you will. It also might mean that you resolved the conflict during the first conversation, but you call or e-mail parents a couple of weeks later to be sure that the conflict has been resolved to their satisfaction. Parents will greatly appreciate the follow-up call because they know that you have taken them seriously and care about their child.

TOOLS FOR SUCCESS

There are times when you communicate with all parents and guardians (i.e., a newsletter), and other times when you communicate with them individually (e.g., by means of e-mails or letters). Both serve very important purposes and are handled very differently. These tools will help you handle both lines of communication. Each of the following templates appears on the CD (see CD, Chapter 9 folder).

Class News Template This template is not designed to show you the layout or decorative nature of a classroom newsletter; it's designed to give you ideas about the content to include in your newsletter. Provide a brief summary of the activities that have been taking place in each content area. In addition, give parents ideas for ways they can follow up on each subject at home. A newsletter emphasizes the importance of the school-home partnership, suggests ways for parents to interact with their children, and thanks parents for specific contributions to the class.

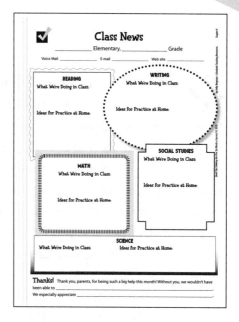

Kelly's Tip

It is important to thank those who support your classroom each month. Be cautious about thanking people by name because you run the risk of failing to thank every person. Instead, make general remarks about events that have taken place: "Thank you to all of the parents who helped with our zoo field trip this month. Thank you to all of the parents who supplied ingredients for our healthy snacks this month."

Kelly's Tip

Depending on the age of your students, consider having them write the newsletter as part of their writing experiences. Assign each content area to a group of students, have them write the article, exchange it with another group to proofread, and then work on polished products. This an excellent, real-life learning experience.

Parent Concern Cheat Sheet It's easy to forget these four important steps for handling conflict when you're wrapped up in a challenging conversation with parents. Make copies of this sheet and keep them in places where you can get to the information quickly to remind yourself of these key ideas.

✓ **Parent Concern Cheat Sheet**

Step 1: LISTEN Listen carefully without interrupting. Take notes if necessary.

Step 2: SUMMARIZE Tell the parents what you have heard to make sure you're talking about the same issue before attempting to develop a resolution.

Step 3: RESPOND If it's a quick fix, respond as appropriate. Otherwise, explain that you'll look into the issue and follow up by a certain time.

Step 4: FOLLOW-UP Be sure to follow up as promised. You might also want to follow up a couple weeks after the issue has been resolved to make sure that things are still going well.

Parent Communication Log Developing strong communication skills is critical and keeping track of conversations with parents is equally important. Each time you communicate with parents, make some quick notes about the conversation so you can refer back to them if you need to. This serves two purposes: First, if a parent contacts you and mentions that you have spoken about this twice before, you can refer back to your Parent Communication Log to review your notes about those conversations. That way, you are prepared for the conversation. Second, if you are working with a struggling student and you've contacted parents several times, you have a record showing the conversations you've had. This will be helpful if you move forward with school-wide interventions. This type of log also comes in handy when you have students who live in two different houses. Sometimes you talk to Mom and other times to Dad. By keeping a log, you have a record of which topics you covered with which parent.

✓	Parent Communication Log				
Date	I Communicated With	About	I Initiated	Parent Initiated	Notes

Quick Tips! Making the First Six Weeks a Success! © 2010 by Kelly Bergman • Scholastic Teaching Resources.   Chapter 9

Kelly's Tip

Decide whether you're going to keep a handwritten log or an electronic one. Keeping an electronic version will allow you to quickly sort the log to find the information you're looking for. Be sure to stay current with your log. It does take a couple of extra minutes, but it will be well worth the time. If you find that you are communicating with certain parents more than others, you might decide to create a separate log for that family so you can access their information as quickly as possible.

Take Action • • • • • • • • • • • •

- Write on your calendar the date when you publish your newsletter each month. Having the date on your calendar each month will remind you to get the newsletter done and be consistent with it.

- Decide who will write your newsletter.

- Develop the format of your newsletter.

- Make several copies of the Parent Concern Cheat Sheet, put them in easily accessible places in your classroom, and keep a copy at home in case you have to return a call from a parent.

- Create your Parent Communication Log. If you're keeping a handwritten log, make copies and put them in a notebook. If you're keeping an electronic log, create the document and save it in an easily accessible place.

- Begin your Parent Communication Log with the phone calls you make to parents during the first two weeks of school (see Chapter 1).

Chapter 10

Be Prepared for Parent Conferences

Scenario A You're preparing to start your fifth parent conference, and they're running 15 minutes late. You're really flustered because the first four conferences didn't go as well as you had hoped. Although you wanted to show parents samples of their children's work, you couldn't put your hands on the work quickly. You're also not sure if you covered every subject, and parents didn't seem very happy when they left. The next parents are coming in the door, and they're already frustrated because you're running so late. What will you do to catch up and gain their trust?

Scenario B You're preparing to start your fifth parent conference, and they're running right on time. You feel great because your first four conferences have gone really well. You have a folder prepared for each student so that you can be sure to cover each subject and show parents samples of their child's work. Parents are complimenting you on several things: your organization and preparation and your knowledge of their children. What a great feeling!

Most parent conferences don't occur within the first six weeks of school, but the preparation for them does. Begin collecting student work samples early in the year so you have several to choose from when it's time for parent conferences.

Tips for Success • • • • • • • • •

Schedule Conferences Begin scheduling parent conferences about three weeks before the date the conferences begin. Check with your teammates to determine how conferences are scheduled. Some schools have one or two people schedule all the conferences for the whole school. Other schools have teachers schedule their own conferences. If you are scheduling your own and you collected time preferences from parents at Back to School Night/Curriculum Night, refer to this information as you create your conference schedule. Send a letter to each family with the time that has been scheduled for them and ask them to confirm that time by returning the form at the bottom of the letter.

Improve attendance at parent conferences by making reminder calls to families one or two days before the conferences. You can ask a parent volunteer to call each family and remind them about the conference.

Paint a Picture of Each Student's Progress Parents want to leave a conference with a clear picture of their child's progress. Each conference should include specific examples and/or samples to illustrate this progress. Be prepared for each conference so that parents know exactly where their child stands. Some students will have made great progress, and you will be celebrating their accomplishments and talking about how you'll continue to challenge them. Some students will have made limited progress, so you'll be recognizing the progress they have made and discussing strategies for helping them progress more quickly.

Make Each Conference Productive Begin each conference by stating something positive (and specific) about the child. For example, you might say, "Johnny does a really nice job of working in groups. He is able to lead his group when he's given that role, and he's also able to follow when someone else is the leader." This sets a very positive tone for the conference.

Next, ask the parents if they have any questions they'd like answered during the conference. Make note of the questions so you can be sure to answer them. Cover each of the subject areas and then refer back to the parents' questions to be sure that they have been answered. Make notes about any questions that were not answered and/or any follow-up that needs to be done.

Kelly's
Tip Set a digital timer at the beginning of each conference. Tell parents that you want to be respectful of their time and also make the most of your time together. Watch the timer and tell parents when you have about five minutes left in the conference. This will help all of you be more aware of time.

Follow Up After Conferences Conferences frequently require some type of follow-up. Perhaps you discussed a strategy, and you told parents you would send home a handout about the strategy. Perhaps you told parents that you would consult a member of the special education team and get back to them. Make notes about the follow-up tasks you need to do and then be sure to complete the tasks. Parents are highly impressed when teachers follow up on their promises, and the trusting relationship that you've worked so hard to establish is maintained.

TOOLS FOR SUCCESS

The level of your preparation for parent conferences will make a strong statement to parents. If you are well organized, parents will leave feeling confident about the information you've provided and have a clear picture of their child's progress. If you are poorly organized, parents will leave feeling frustrated about the lack of clear information. These tools will help you be fully prepared for conferences. Each of the following templates appears on the CD (see CD, Chapter 10 folder).

Parent Conference Checklist Use this checklist to gather the information and materials you need for conferences. The last item on the checklist suggests that you prepare copies of handouts that parents may request during conferences. Having these readily available means that there will be fewer tasks to follow up with. For instance, if you're discussing math facts during the conference and parents ask for practice sheets, you can give them copies right then and not have to send them home later.

Parent Conference Letter Send this letter home to parents 3–4 weeks before conferences. The letter tells parents what they can expect at the conference and asks them to confirm that they will be able to attend. The letter is written to remind parents that this is a time for parents to talk with the teacher and reminds them to make child-care arrangements. If you are having student-led conferences, remind parents to leave siblings at home so they can focus on this child.

Parent Conference Scheduling Form Different schools have different schedules for conferences. Check with your office staff to see if there is a school-wide system for scheduling conferences. If not, use the template on the CD as a starting point and modify it as you need to. Schedule breaks to use the restroom and get a drink of water. You can also use a break to catch up if you fall behind: cut a 15-minute break to five minutes. This will still allow you time for the restroom and a drink of water.

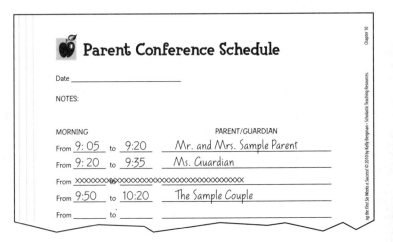

✔ Parent Conference Planning Sheet Use this sheet to help you prepare for each parent conference so that you can paint a picture of each student's progress. The first section has a place to write the positive feedback that you will share with parents to begin the conference. The next section provides space for you to note parent questions during the conference. Complete the sections about the student's strengths and goals for reading, writing, math, social studies, and science before the parent conferences begin. Also make notes about the student's behavior and social skills. As you prepare the planning sheet for each student, be sure to review your Parent Communication Log to refresh your memory about previous contact you've had with parents. Make some notes on the back of the page if there are things you want to remember to discuss. Put a star on the corner of the front page to remind you about any notes you've made on the back. You will also want to review the file you created for each student (see Chapter 2). This is the time to review notes from parents, clinic passes, and other items from those files to see if there are any other issues that need to be addressed. During the conference, make notes in the last section about any follow-up tasks that you need to do.

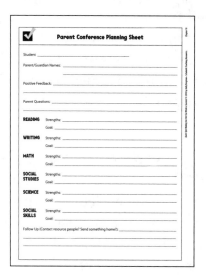

Kelly's
Tip As you prepare the Parent Conference Planning Sheet for each student, collect work samples that demonstrate the points you are making. Place them in a folder with the child's name on it. When the planning sheet is complete, place it on top inside the folder, and you are fully prepared for the conference. You will be able to open the folder, begin the conference, follow an organized agenda, and quickly show examples of student work. Send the work home with parents.

Kelly's
Tip After you have completed all the parent conferences, review each planning sheet to see what notes you made. Look carefully at the "Follow Up" section and make a list of all the tasks you need to do to follow up on conferences. Try to get all these tasks done within a week after finishing the conferences. Once you're finished with the planning sheets, file them in each child's individual folder so you can refer back to them when it's time for parent conferences in the spring (see Chapter 2).

Spelling Words Study Tips Conferences also frequently include a conversation about helping students study for spelling tests. Have copies of this handout available to give to parents. You could also distribute it at Back to School Night/Curriculum Night (see Chapter 7).

Reading Strategies Study Tips Have copies of this handout ready to give to parents. These strategies come naturally to teachers, but parents will really appreciate having ideas for reading with their children. This handout could also be distributed at Back to School Night/Curriculum Night (see Chapter 7).

Math Facts Study Tips Students must master basic math facts in order to do more complex math operations. There is not much time during a school day to practice facts, so most of the practice needs to be done at home. Most parents are anxious to help their children improve their math facts but need some ideas for ways to practice. These tips could also be distributed at Back to School Night/Curriculum Night (see Chapter 7).

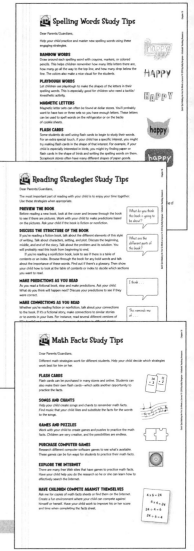

Take Action • • • • • • • • • • •

- ■ If you collected time preferences from parents at Back to School Night/Curriculum Night, refer to those when scheduling conferences.

- ■ Send a Parent Conference Letter to each family.

- ■ Complete a Parent Conference Planning Sheet for each student, collect work samples, and create a folder for each student.

- ■ Ask a parent volunteer to make reminder calls two days before conferences.

- ■ Prepare a waiting area according to the Parent Conference Checklist.

- ■ Prepare conference area according to the Parent Conference Checklist.

Kelly's
Tip Homework is often a topic of conversation during conferences. Have copies of the Homework Tips sheet (see Chapter 4) available to give to parents if the topic comes up. Being able to give parents the handout during the conference means one less task for you to follow up on. This handout could also be distributed at Back to School Night/Curriculum Night (see Chapter 7).

Spelling Words Study Tips

Dear Parents/Guardians,

Help your child practice and master new spelling words using these engaging strategies.

RAINBOW WORDS

Draw around each spelling word with crayons, markers, or colored pencils. This helps children remember how many little letters there are, how many go all the way to the top line, and how many drop below the line. The colors also make a nice visual for the students.

PLAYDOUGH WORDS

Let children use playdough to make the shapes of the letters in their spelling words. This is especially good for children who need a tactile/kinesthetic activity.

MAGNETIC LETTERS

Magnetic letter sets can often be found at dollar stores. You'll probably want to have two or three sets so you have enough letters. These letters can be used to spell words on the refrigerator or on the backs of cookie sheets.

FLASH CARDS

Some students do well using flash cards to begin to study their words. For an extra special touch, if your child has a specific interest, you might try making flash cards in the shape of that interest. For example, if your child is especially interested in birds, you might try finding paper or flash cards in the shape of birds and writing the spelling words on them. Scrapbook stores often have many different shapes of paper goods.

SALTY FINGERS

Fill a 9-inch by 13-inch pan with salt or sand (sugar gets too sticky) and have your child use his or her fingers to practice spelling the words. This is another good one for tactile/kinesthetic learners.

ACRONYMS

Some children have a hard time memorizing spelling words, but they do really well with acronyms. If you find that your child is having difficulty with particular words, have him or her make up an acronym for the word. For example, if your child has trouble with the word "because," you might work together to come up with an acronym such as the following: Bobby's Elves Crave Aunt Ursula's Scrambled Eggs.

Reading Strategies Study Tips

Dear Parents/Guardians,

The most important part of reading with your child is to enjoy your time together. Use these strategies when appropriate.

PREVIEW THE BOOK

Before reading a new book, look at the cover and browse through the book to see if there are pictures. Work with your child to make predictions based on the pictures. Ask your child if the book is fiction or nonfiction.

> What do you think this book is going to be about?

DISCUSS THE STRUCTURE OF THE BOOK

If you're reading a fiction book, talk about the different elements of this style of writing. Talk about characters, setting, and plot. Discuss the beginning, middle, and end of the story. Talk about the problem and its solution. You will probably read this book from beginning to end.

> What are the different parts of this book?

If you're reading a nonfiction book, look to see if there is a table of contents or an index. Browse through the book for any bold words and talk about the importance of these words. Find out if there's a glossary. Then show your child how to look at the table of contents or index to decide which sections you want to read.

MAKE PREDICTIONS AS YOU READ

As you read a fictional book, stop and make predictions. Ask your child: What do you think will happen next? Discuss your predictions to see if they were correct.

> I think . . .

MAKE CONNECTIONS AS YOU READ

Whether you're reading fiction or nonfiction, talk about your connections to the book. If it's a fictional story, make connections to similar stories or to events in your lives. For instance, read several different versions of "Cinderella" and compare them. Compare characters in different stories. If it's a nonfiction text, make connections to similar topics. For instance, if you're reading a book about bears, compare that to a book you've read about beavers. If you're reading a book about Africa, compare that to a book you've read about Germany.

> This reminds me of . . .

RETELL THE STORY OR RESTATE THE FACTS

When reading a fictional story, stop every now and then to retell the story. You want your child to be able to make movies of the story in his or her head as he or she reads. Drawing pictures of the story might help with the retelling.

> This story was about . . .

When reading a nonfiction text, stop every now and then to restate the facts. What have you learned as you've been reading? What important words have you learned? Draw pictures to represent the important vocabulary words.

Math Facts Study Tips

Dear Parents/Guardians,

Different math strategies work for different students. Help your child decide which strategies work best for him or her.

FLASH CARDS
Flash cards can be purchased in many stores and online. Students can also make their own flash cards—which adds another opportunity to practice the facts.

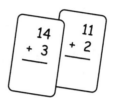

SONGS AND CHANTS
Help your child create songs and chants to remember math facts. Find music that your child likes and substitute the facts for the words to the songs.

GAMES AND PUZZLES
Work with your child to create games and puzzles to practice the math facts. Children are very creative, and the possibilities are endless.

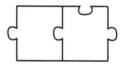

PURCHASE COMPUTER GAMES
Research different computer software games to see what's available. These games can be fun ways for students to practice their math facts.

EXPLORE THE INTERNET
There are many free Web sites that have games to practice math facts. Have your child help you do the research so he or she can learn how to effectively search the Internet.

HAVE CHILDREN COMPETE AGAINST THEMSELVES
Ask me for copies of math facts sheets or find them on the Internet. Create a fun environment where your child can compete against himself or herself. Have your child work to improve his or her score and time when completing the facts sheet.

$4 \times 6 = 24$

$6 \times 4 = 24$

$24 \div 4 = 6$

$24 \div 6 = 4$

Appendix

Graphic Organizers and Instructional Strategies

STRATEGY: COMPARING AND CONTRASTING

Venn Diagram
Triple Venn Diagram
Comparison Matrix

STRATEGY: BRAINSTORMING

Web

STRATEGY: ASSESSING PRIOR KNOWLEDGE

KWL Chart

STRATEGY: DIFFERENTIATION

Activity Menu

Activity menus are great for allowing students to work at their own pace and level and can be used in a variety of ways. Here are some ideas to start with:

- *Different Levels of Thinking* Designate each row to a different level of thinking, as shown at right. Have students choose one activity from each row.
- *Six Traits of Writing* Write a trait in each box and an activity for that trait. Have students select four activities to do with their piece of writing.
- *Areas of Intelligence* Write an area of intelligence in each box with an activity that supports that area of intelligence. Have students select four activities to complete. (For more information, see Howard Gardner's work on multiple intelligences.)

Activity Menu

Place a checkmark in the activities you want to do.

Application ☐ Apply this to something else.	Application ☐ Demonstrate your learning.	Application ☐ Show how this works.
Analysis ☐ Break this down into smaller parts.	Analysis ☐ Draw a diagram to show this.	Analysis ☐ Illustrate this.
Evaluation ☐ Compare this to something else.	Evaluation ☐ Critique this.	Evaluation ☐ Summarize this.

I agree to complete the activities that are checked above.

Name: ____________________

Date Received: __________ Date Completed: __________

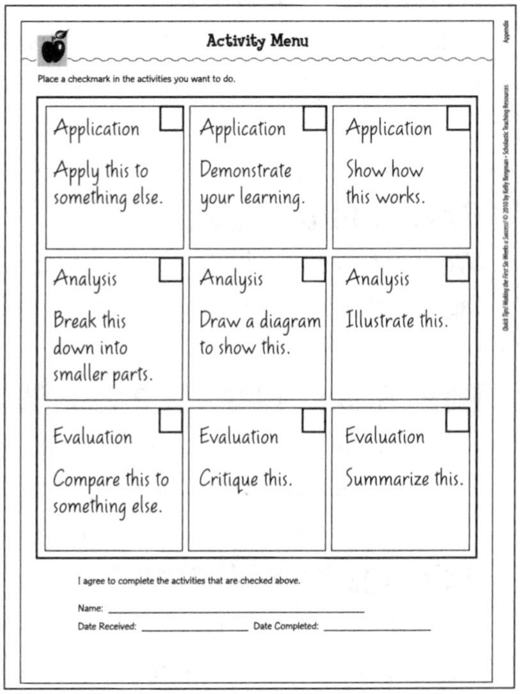

STRATEGY: PROOFREADING AND EDITING

Use these checklists as a starting point for having your students edit and proofread their writing. The first part of the checklists includes writing skills appropriate for the grade level. The second section includes the six traits of writing.

Venn Diagram

Name

Date

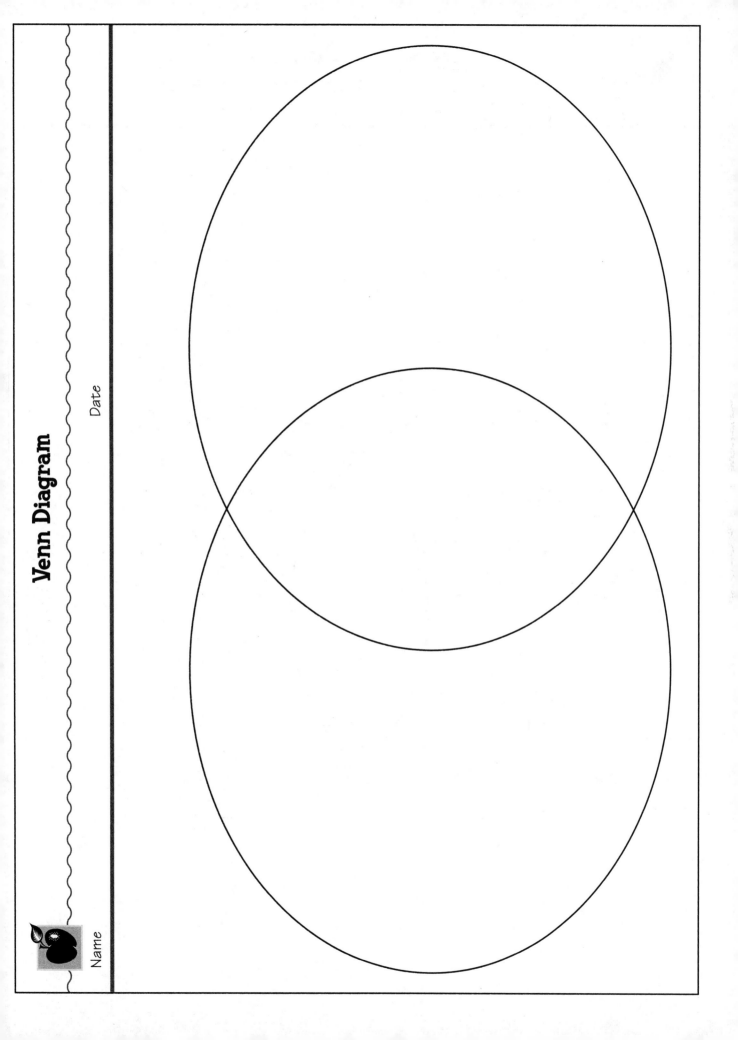

Triple Venn Diagram

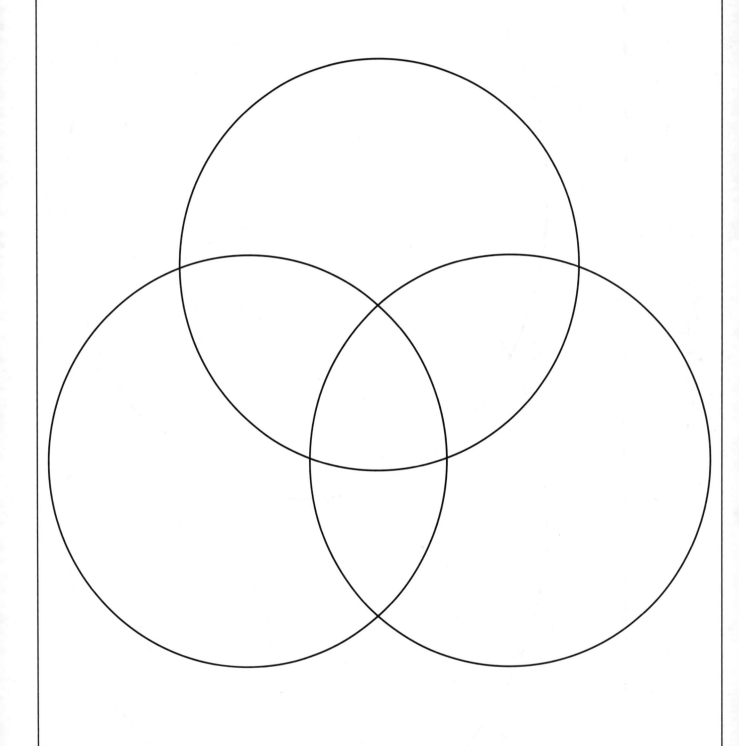

Comparison Matrix

Name

Date

CHARACTERISTICS TO BE COMPARED

ITEMS TO COMPARE

Web

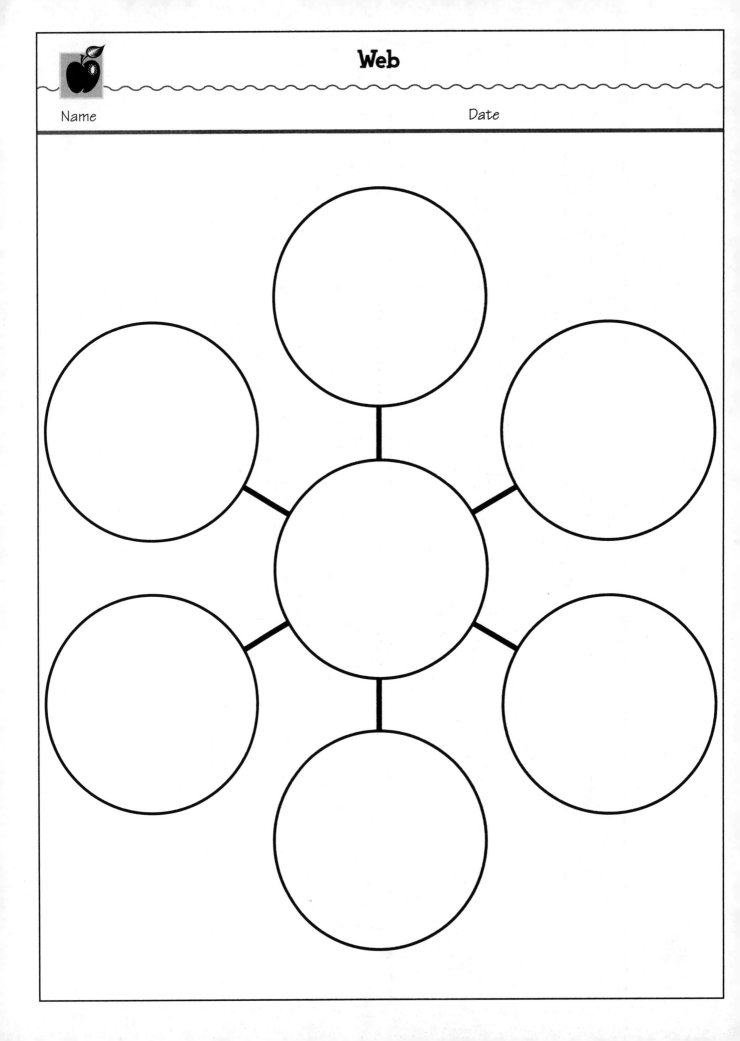

KWL Chart

Topic

K	W	L
What do you know about this topic?	What do you want to know about this topic?	What did you learn about this topic?

Activity Menu

Place a checkmark in the activities you want to do.

I agree to complete the activities that are checked above.

Name: _____

Date Received: _____ Date Completed: _____

Writing Checklist—Grade 1

Name _____   Date _____

Y = Yes

N = No

STUDENT		TEACHER
_____	Correct Heading	_____
_____	Clean Notebook Paper	_____
_____	Written in Pencil	_____
_____	Neat Handwriting	_____
_____	Complete Sentences	_____
_____	Periods	_____
_____	Capital Letters	_____

Writing Traits

_____	Ideas and Content	_____
_____	Organization	_____
_____	Voice	_____
_____	Word Choice	_____
_____	Sentence Fluency	_____
_____	Conventions	_____

Writing Checklist—Grade 2

Name _____ **Date** _____

+ = almost always used   **/** = used sometimes

– = needs improvement   **NA** = not applicable for this assignment

STUDENT		TEACHER
_____	Correct Heading	_____
_____	Clean Notebook Paper	_____
_____	Written in Pencil	_____
_____	Neat Handwriting	_____
_____	Double-Spaced Draft	_____
_____	Complete Sentences	_____
_____	Priority Spelling	_____
	(includes sight words and frequently used words appropriate to grade level)	
_____	Punctuation Checked	_____
_____	Capitalization Checked	_____

Writing Traits

STUDENT		TEACHER
_____	Ideas and Content	_____
_____	Organization	_____
_____	Voice	_____
_____	Word Choice	_____
_____	Sentence Fluency	_____
_____	Conventions	_____

Writing Checklist—Grade 3

Name _____   Date _____

+ = almost always used   **/** = used sometimes

— = needs improvement   **NA** = not applicable for this assignment

STUDENT		TEACHER
_____	Correct Heading	_____
_____	Clean Notebook Paper	_____
_____	Written in Pencil	_____
_____	Neat Handwriting	_____
_____	Double-Spaced Draft	_____
_____	Complete Sentences	_____
_____	Priority Spelling	_____
	(includes sight words and frequently used words appropriate to grade level)	
_____	Punctuation Checked	_____
_____	Capitalization Checked	_____
_____	Margins Used	_____
_____	Paragraphs Indented	_____

Writing Traits

STUDENT		TEACHER
_____	Ideas and Content	_____
_____	Organization	_____
_____	Voice	_____
_____	Word Choice	_____
_____	Sentence Fluency	_____
_____	Conventions	_____

Writing Checklist—Grades 4-5

+ = almost always used   **/** = used sometimes

— = needs improvement   **NA** = not applicable for this assignment

STUDENT		TEACHER
_____	Correct Heading	_____
_____	Clean Notebook Paper	_____
_____	Written in Pencil	_____
_____	Neat Handwriting	_____
_____	Double-Spaced Draft	_____
_____	Complete Sentences	_____
_____	Priority Spelling	_____

(includes sight words and frequently used words
appropriate to grade level)

STUDENT		TEACHER
_____	Punctuation Checked	_____
_____	Capitalization Checked	_____
_____	Margins Used	_____
_____	Paragraphs Indented	_____
_____	Written in Cursive	_____

Writing Traits

STUDENT		TEACHER
_____	Ideas and Content	_____
_____	Organization	_____
_____	Voice	_____
_____	Word Choice	_____
_____	Sentence Fluency	_____
_____	Conventions	_____